Elite • 143

Canadian Airborne Forces since 1942

Bernd Horn & Michel Wyczynski • Illustrated by C Chagas

Consultant editor Martin Windrow

First published in Great Britain in 2006 by Osprey Publishing,
Midland House, West Way, Botley, Oxford OX2 0PH, UK
443 Park Avenue South, New York, NY 10016, USA

Email: info@ospreypublishing.com

© 2006 Osprey Publishing Ltd.

ISBN-10: 1 84176 985 1
ISBN-13: 978 1 84176 985 1

Editor: Martin Windrow
Page layouts by Alan Hamp
Index by Alison Worthington
Originated by United Graphics Pte Ltd, Singapore
Printed in China through World Print Ltd.

06 07 08 09 10   10 9 8 7 6 5 4 3 2 1

A CIP catalogue record for this book is available from the British Library

FOR A CATALOGUE OF ALL BOOKS PUBLISHED BY
OSPREY MILITARY AND AVIATION PLEASE CONTACT:
North America:
Osprey Direct, c/o Random House Distribution Center, 400 Hahn Road,
Westminster, MD 21157
Email: info@ospreydirect.com

All other regions:
Osprey Direct UK PO Box 140, Wellingborough, Northants, NN8 2FA, UK
Email: info@ospreydirect.co.uk

Buy online at www.ospreypublishing.com

Artist's Note

Readers may care to note that the original paintings from which the
colour plates in this book were prepared are available for private
sale. All reproduction copyright whatsoever is retained by the
Publishers. All enquiries should be addressed to:

Carlos Chagas mail to:crchagas@terra.com.br

The Publishers regret that they can enter into no correspondence
upon this matter.

Acknowledgments

The authors are most grateful to Ed Storey and Daniel Côté for their
assistance during the preparation of this study.

CANADIAN AIRBORNE FORCES SINCE 1942

RELUCTANT BEGINNINGS

Cpl Frederick G. Topham, a medical orderly with 1st Canadian Parachute Battalion, was awarded the Victoria Cross for gallantry above and beyond the call of duty on 24 March 1945, when the battalion was fighting off German attacks on a drop zone east of the Rhine during Operation 'Varsity'. The battalion's yellow shoulder strap loop is just visible at far left. (Private collection)

THE GERMAN INVASION of Western Europe on 10 May 1940 caught the Allies by surprise in more ways than one. The Blitzkrieg, relying upon speed, firepower, mechanized forces and combined operations, included such innovations as airborne assault. The defenders of France and the Low Countries were rapidly overwhelmed, and almost overnight the British, their few remaining allies, and the watching world came to realize that their warfighting methodology was defunct.

Canada was no different: the country was totally unprepared for modern war. At the start of the conflict the Canadian Army mustered a mere 4,261 regular force personnel, with an additional 51,000 Non-Permanent Active Militia members (i.e. reservists) scattered across the country. But manpower was not the only problem: the Army was devoid of even the most rudimentary equipment. It possessed only four anti-aircraft guns, five mortars, 82 Vickers medium machine guns, 10 Bren light machine guns and two light tanks. Needless to say, the idea of parachute troops was not even considered. In this respect Canada was no different from Britain and the United States; during the interwar years very few nations, with the exception of the Russians and the Germans, had seriously invested energy or resources in the concept of airborne forces.[1]

Following the results obtained by the German utilization of paratroopers and glider troops at the spearhead of their invading forces in Holland and Belgium, a wave of airborne paranoia swept over Britain and other nations. The spectre of airborne soldiers descending into areas previously considered safe was keenly felt. Even the combative and tough-spirited British Prime Minister, Winston Churchill, was shaken by the apparent prospect of a German invasion of southern England spearheaded by 30,000 Fallschirmjäger; this overestimated the strength of 7. Flieger Division by two hundred per cent, but parachute units were indeed given an important part to play in the contingency plans for Operation 'Sealion'.

1 See Elite 136, *World War II Airborne Warfare Tactics*

The parachute scare had a particular resonance for Canada. The precipitate British withdrawal from the European continent under the pressure of the German juggernaut forced the abandonment of most of the British Expeditionary Force's equipment on the beaches of northern France. As a result, the unblooded Canadian troops who had already arrived in England found themselves to be the best equipped and organized to fight and, unsurprisingly, they were given a key role in the planned defence of southern England. The need to defend against the airborne menace became one of their pre-eminent concerns.

The pervading fear that the mere threat of German paratroopers instilled in Britain was not lost on the Canadians, particularly Col E.L.M.Burns, a staff officer who redeployed to Canada to assist with the creation of a modern Canadian army. He quickly grasped the strategic value of airborne forces, and realized their efficacy at striking the enemy's command and logistical facilities located behind the front lines. He fully understood their effect in psychologically dislocating their opponents' front-line combat forces. Paratroopers, Burns realized, were a very potent offensive force that made the concept of a safe rear area obsolete.

Upon his return to Canada in July 1940, Burns immediately recommended the creation of a distinct parachute force for the Canadian Army. However, his repeated efforts failed. The distant and myopic Canadian senior military leadership saw no purpose for parachutists in the defence of Canada or – more surprisingly – for an overseas role. The concept of 'special troops' was alien and distasteful to a senior Canadian military leadership who were wrestling with the dichotomy between their experience and understanding of war and the reality that now stared them in the face. Their immediate preoccupation was transforming the long-neglected Army into a modern organization capable of defeating the Germans.

Supply shortfalls dictated the continued use of American equipment even at the A-35 Canadian Parachute Training Centre (CPTC). Here candidates for the Canadian parachute training course are seen wearing the US Army's M-1942 parachutist's uniform, the M-1 steel helmet with the M-1C airborne liner and strapping, and Corcoran jump boots; they are buckling on American T-5 parachutes. (Courtesy 1st Canadian Parachute Battalion Association Archives)

Of equal concern to them was the realization that any type of special troops such as paratroopers – because of the limited numbers Canada could generate, and the very specific operational role they would perform – would most likely be placed under British command. For the Canadian political and military leadership the question of Canadian control of Canadian troops, which had its roots in the Boer War and had been so stubbornly argued in World War I, was a central issue that was not to be easily dismissed.[2]

Nonetheless, as is most often the case with smaller powers, the decisions of its allies had a significant effect on Canadian thinking. As early as June 1940, Churchill demanded the establishment of a British corps 'of parachute troops on a scale of equal to five thousand.' Churchill's direction was initially resisted, as British commanders were more concerned with building up their savaged forces to defend England and vital overseas possessions. However, the sucessful (if costly) invasion of the island of Crete by German airborne forces in May 1941 seemed to break the institutional resistance to parachute troops, and by the spring of 1942 both the British and Americans fully embraced the concept of airborne forces. As the balance of the war began to shift in favour of the Allies, the focus swung from a concentration on defence to means of offence, and nothing embodied raw, aggressive offensive more than paratroops. Very quickly, airborne troops became a defining component of a modern army. Not to be left out, senior Canadian military commanders reversed their earlier reservations and recommended the establishment of a parachute battalion to J.L.Ralston, the Minister of National Defence (MND).

Initial training

The minister readily agreed, and on 1 July 1942 the Canadian War Cabinet Committee approved the formation of a parachute unit. However, the committee clearly stated that the purpose of the paratroops was home defence, specifically for the recapture of lost airfields or reinforcement of remote localities – a policy diametrically opposed to earlier military estimates that rejected the need for airborne forces to fill that role. It also ignored the changing tide of the war, which now placed the Allies on the offensive and removed any likelihood of an attack on Canada.

Nonetheless, once authority was given the Army quickly took action. That summer 85 selected officers and non-commissioned officers serving overseas were sent to the parachute training school at RAF Station Ringway in England. Similarly, in mid-August 1942 a group of 27 intrepid volunteers under the command of Maj H.D.Proctor deployed from Canada to Fort Benning, Georgia, to commence American parachute training. In total, these individuals represented the embryo of what would become the 1st Canadian Parachute Battalion, forming the initial training cadre that would instruct those who followed. Simultaneously with these developments, an effort was made to begin recruiting for the battalion at large. Messages were quickly sent to all Military Districts across Canada calling for volunteers to fill the ranks of the planned 616-man unit.

At the core of the Canadian airborne programme was a desire on the part of the senior Canadian Army leadership to develop a distinct

Canadian approach, combining the best of both British and American methods and practice. To this end, on 25 July 1942 an Inter-Service Committee selected Camp Shilo, Manitoba, as the future site for the national parachute training centre. Despite these good intentions, however, there was little time and few resources to spare. Therefore, concurrently with the construction of the centre, National Defence Headquarters (NDHQ) reached an agreement with the US authorities to send the rapidly growing group of Canadian volunteers to Fort Benning for parachute instruction. This served two functions: it allowed for immediate training of volunteers, and also provided the opportunity to conduct further research into the necessary and best types of facilities and equipment required to establish the Canadian parachute training school in Shilo.

Although the Canadian Army was late in creating a parachute capability, it now made a concerted effort to develop its airborne programme. Finding the necessary raw manpower was not a problem: volunteers poured in from across Canada and from units serving overseas in Britain. Unsurprisingly, however, it quickly became evident that not everyone was capable of becoming a paratrooper. On average only some 50 per cent of volunteers passed the initial screening process. Of these successful candidates, another 30–35 per cent were winnowed out during the training, which was designed to develop an exceptionally high level of physical fitness, as well as to test the personal courage and motivation of the volunteers.

1st CANADIAN PARACHUTE BATTALION, 1942–44

Growing pains

In late September 1942 LtCol G.F.P.Bradbrooke was appointed commanding officer of 1st Canadian Parachute Battalion (1 Cdn Para Bn), and was immediately faced with the task of establishing a unit from scratch. This would be challenging under the best of conditions, due to the normal administrative and operational problems related to recruiting the right type of personnel, as well as locating and ordering the required equipment, infrastructure and weaponry – and it all had to be accomplished under the pressures and scarcities of war. Moreover, Bradbrooke was required to prepare and train a unit for an entirely new form of warfare that was not yet fully understood.

Adding to the difficulties of establishing the new unit was another dilemma. In July 1942 the War Cabinet also authorized a second unit, officially designated the 2nd Canadian Parachute Battalion. This name, however, was misleading. It was not a parachute battalion at all, but rather a commando unit. The designation was assigned for security reasons to cover the true nature of its operational mandate. On 25 May 1943 the name was changed to reflect this, to 1st Canadian Special Service Battalion; this in fact represented the Canadian element of the joint US/Canadian First Special Service Force (FSSF). Of immediate impact on the formation of 1 Cdn Para Bn was this other unit's higher priority for scarce resources, including high quality manpower, which created a grave problem for LtCol Bradbrooke. The NDHQ directed him to transfer all jump-qualified personnel who volunteered to 2 Cdn Para Bn; and a rumour that this supposed sister unit would see action before 1 Cdn Para Bn quickly circulated through the ranks. Predictably, many of the most aggressive and motivated paratroopers became frustrated with their battalion's seemingly slow activation, and transferred to the 2nd Battalion.

The loss of qualified paratroopers was only one of 1 Cdn Para Bn's growing pains, and a more ominous problem soon faced LtCol Bradbrooke. In the fall of 1942 morale plummeted when the senior military leadership decided that conscripts drafted into the Army under the National Resources Mobilization Act (NRMA) were entitled to join the parachute battalion. This infuriated the paratroopers: the inclusion of these soldiers implied that the battalion would never see active duty overseas, because NRMA personnel were designated for Home Defence service only. Fortunately, the crisis was quickly averted. Senior staff in Ottawa, as well as the officers charged with the discipline and training of 1 Cdn Para Bn, immediately advised the Chief of the General Staff (CGS) that the inclusion of NRMA personnel was sending the wrong message and causing serious recruiting and retention problems. The problem was quickly rectified by an announcement from the CGS that 'all parachute volunteers for the 1 Cdn Para Bn must be active personnel'.

By the end of December 1942, most of the early problems seemed to have dissipated. 'We feel confident that the New Year will see fulfilment of the original NDHQ plans', revealed a War Diary entry, 'and the Battalion will be distinguished when called into active combat overseas'. These words appeared to be prophetic. The unit was beginning to benefit from a sense of cohesiveness that proved stronger than subsequent calls for transfers to the FSSF. In addition, challenging training and a steady influx of equipment was building a distinct sense of confidence and unit pride.

A-35 CPTC, Shilo, Manitoba, winter 1944: upon completion of the four-week parachute course, candidates moved on to the ground warfare training phase. Once again, due to the delay in making available to trainees some equipment employed by the battalion in Europe, they had to use the regular Mk II helmet. (Courtesy Library and Archives Canada (LAC), PA-209731)

Organization

The war establishment of the battalion was set at 616 all ranks (26 officers, 73 senior NCOs and 517 rank and file), within four sub-units that broke down as follows:

Headquarters Company (5 officers, 20 SNCOs & 144 men), consisting of: Battalion HQ; Company HQ; Signals Platoon; Administrative Platoon (with 77 personnel, this was the largest platoon in the unit); Mortar Platoon (4x 3in mortar detachments); Protection Section; Intelligence Section.

Three *Rifle Companies* (each 5 officers, 16 SNCOs & 118 men), each consisting of: Company HQ, with 2x 3in mortar detachments and an Anti-Tank Section; and three Rifle Platoons (1 officer, 4 SNCOs & 29 men), each consisting of Platoon HQ and three Rifle Sections.

Major weapon holdings for the battalion were established at 29x light machine guns (Bren guns); 10x 3in mortars; 28x 2in mortars; and 10x Boys .55in AT rifles – later replaced with the Projector Infantry Anti-Tank (PIAT). Not surprisingly, many of these support weapons were often brigaded to give the unit greater flexibility and firepower during operations.

Training in Canada

On 15 April 1943 the battalion reported to its new home at Shilo, Manitoba. With the opening there of the S-14 Canadian Parachute Training School, the battalion could now meet all its training requirements at home. By now the paratroopers were growing restless. To a man, they had volunteered for airborne service in order to see combat as quickly as possible, and all yearned for the chance to take the fight to the enemy. In this vane, LtCol Bradbrooke publicly announced that his paratroopers were 'the tip of the spear'. Their role in the offensive against the enemy was clear: 'They must expect to go in first... to penetrate behind enemy lines and to fight in isolated positions.' He designed their training accordingly.

Colonel Bradbrooke's focus was on infantry battle-drills, weapons handling, parachute training, and physical fitness. Route marches became a dreaded component of the training plan. Demanding and gruelling training, which stressed psychological as well as physical strength, conferred on the paratroopers a sense that they were becoming different from the other members of the Canadian Army – and they were. Compared with regular infantry, airborne soldiers were required to operate on their own, often behind enemy lines, with no secure rear area and with limited firepower, supplies and ammunition. The paratroopers would

As part of British 6th Airborne Division, all 1 Cdn Para Bn personnel were required to undergo a conversion course at the Central Landing Establishment, RAF Ringway, to familiarize them with the British X-Type parachute. At Ringway the Canadians wore the canvas-and-Sorbo rubber training helmet, the sleeveless green 'jacket, parachutist's, 1942 pattern', the Denison smock, black ammunition boots and webbing anklets.
(Photographer Sgt E.R.Bonter, LAC, PA-205330)

have to rely on their physical fitness, aggression, marksmanship, stealth and tenacity to hold their ground until the main force could link up with them. The impact of the physically and mentally demanding training soon became evident. It forged a distinct identity and gave life to a reputation for aggressiveness, courage and toughness.

Overseas at last

As training progressed, the senior command at NDHQ struggled with the issue of the battalion's employment. Clearly, a collection of aggressive and offensive-minded paratroopers would be wasted on Home Defence tasks, particularly as there was no direct threat to Canada. Therefore, even before the paratroopers were considered operationally ready, they were offered to the Commander of Home Forces in England – an offer that was quickly and gratefully accepted. Consequently, in March 1943 it was announced that 1 Cdn Para Bn would be included in the order of battle of a second British airborne division that was in the process of forming.

Despite its spirit, the battalion was in fact not yet ready for combat. It had not completed collective training, and even the most optimistic observers believed that it would require a further two months of preparation before becoming fully operational. Although reinforcements required to bring the battalion up to strength were continually arriving from the now-renamed A-35 Canadian Parachute Training Centre, there was still a shortage of trained troops. This shortfall would naturally become even more pronounced once the unit was involved in combat. Therefore, recognizing both this reality and the exacting training requirements for a specialist parachute unit, NDHQ established a special Parachute Training Company, with the specific mandate to train and provide qualified paratroopers as reinforcements for 1 Cdn Para Bn; this was later expanded to an entire 1 Canadian Parachute Training Battalion.

In late June 1943 the long wait came to an end. The battalion's 31 officers and 548 other ranks deployed from Halifax on board the *Queen Elizabeth* for overseas duty. The paratroopers subsequently disembarked at Greenock, Scotland, on 28 July. On arrival they were attached to the 3rd Parachute Brigade (3 Para Bde), as part of the 6th Airborne Division. The battalion rapidly settled into their quarters at Carter Barracks in Bulford Camp, Wiltshire, and their training began in earnest once again.

Their new brigade commander was the incomparable Brig James Hill, an experienced paratroop officer who had seen combat in Tunisia as CO of the British 1st Parachute Battalion following the Allied landings in French North Africa. While in North Africa he was severely wounded and evacuated to England. Based on his operational

Wearing the canvas-and-rubber training helmet and the X-Type parachute, a soldier of 1 Cdn Para Bn jumps from a C-47 Dakota. The British parachute used a 'canopy last' system which gave less of an opening shock, but the 'canopy first' American rigs could be jumped with greater safety from lower altitudes. Note that the British did not use a reserve pack on the chest. (Photographer Sgt E.R.Bonter, LAC, PA-115865)

experience, Hill believed that the gruelling nature of airborne warfare was such that the survival of his paratroopers depended to a great extent on their physical fitness. He set demanding standards: Brig Hill expected a unit to cover 50 miles in 18 hours with each soldier carrying a 60lb pack and his weapon, and 10-mile marches within a two-hour limit were considered the norm.

In combination with fitness training, the initial two months in England also focused on weapons handling and specialist training. Only when a sound foundation of individual skills had been laid did the battalion and brigade concentrate on collective training. In this regard the battalion's continual improvement was not lost on their brigade commander. In early February 1944, during an exercise that simulated an invasion of Europe, Hill wrote: 'I feel I must write and congratulate you on the excellent show your battalion put up from the Albemarles on Exercise 'Co-operation'... If [1 Cdn Para Bn] continue to make progress in this connection at this rate, they will soon be the best jumping exponents in our airborne corps and I should very much like to see them achieve this end for themselves. Well done.'

INTO BATTLE, 1944–45

The Normandy invasion

By spring 1944 it was merely a matter of time before the Canadian paratroopers would be tested in battle; the storming of Hitler's *Festung Europa* was close at hand. The planning and preparation for the invasion of Europe was now in the final stages, and missions had already been assigned.

The British 6th Airborne Division would be responsible for protecting the east or left flank of the British 3rd Infantry Division, which was to land on Sword Beach west of the little seaside resort of Ouistreham. In their turn, 3 Para Bde were given a daunting series of tasks: destroying the coastal defence battery at Merville, demolishing the bridges over the River Dives in the area of Cabourg and Troarn, and controlling the high ridge centred on the small village of Le Mesnil that dominated the landing beaches from the east. Moreover, Le Mesnil was a vital crossroads on the Cabourg–Caen highway, and thus critical for German efforts to manoeuvre in response to the invasion. The brigade also had the additional responsibility of harassing and disrupting the German lines of communication and defensive efforts to the greatest extent possible.

Brigadier Hill assigned 1 Cdn Para Bn the responsibility of covering the left flank of the brigade's drop zone and protecting its movements within the DZ. The battalion was also given three primary missions to be carried out in the eastern and central areas of the Robehomme–Varaville–Le Mesnil sector. The battalion's A Company was responsible for the defence and protection of 9 Para Bn's left flank during its approach march and attack on the Merville battery. Meanwhile B Coy, with one section of the Para Engineer Sqn, were tasked to blow up two bridges spanning the River Dives. Initially C Coy was given a Pathfinder mission; thereafter it was to destroy a German headquarters and bridge, as well as neutralizing enemy positions at Varaville.

At 2230 hours on 5 June 1944, members of C Coy, 1 Cdn Para Bn emplaned in Albemarles and left from Harwell airfield to commence the liberation of Occupied Europe. These paratroopers were part of the invasion Pathfinder element tasked with locating, securing and preparing the DZs for the main airborne assault. The remainder of the battalion proceeded to Down Ampney airfield and emplaned in Douglas C-47 Dakotas; they were in the air by 2300 hours. The nation's first paratroopers were about to write a new page in Canadian military history, founding what would become a proud airborne tradition.

The battalion crossed the Channel, and jumped into France between 0030 hours and 0130 hours on 6 June. Like those of virtually all the Allied airborne units that night, the Canadian drops were badly scattered over a wide area as a result of the lack of navigational aids, and of the thick dust and smoke that drifted over the drop zones from the heavy bombing of nearby targets. Heavy enemy anti-aircraft fire also panicked many of the pilots into taking immediate evasive action, which only magnified the difficulty of delivering the paratroopers accurately to their objectives. On the first drop alone, only 30 of a possible 110 paratroopers of C Coy landed on their DZ, and the subsequent drops were no better: the second group, made up of the main body of the battalion, was scattered over an area 40 times greater than planned. To add to the problems, many of the extra leg-bags that the men were carrying ripped open with the shock of parachute opening, scattering the unit's vital heavy machine guns, mortars and anti-tank weapons across the Normandy countryside. This significantly reduced the firepower available to the airborne soldiers in the critical days that followed.

In the midst of this growing chaos, the physical and psychological toughness honed by careful training showed its value. The paratroopers, as individuals and as a unit, not only persevered but actually flourished despite the unexpected situations and set-backs. By the end of the day their resilience had enabled them to attain all their assigned objectives – with less than 30 per cent of the troops and equipment originally allocated to these tasks. Having completed their allotted missions, the sur-viving paratroopers dug in to hold the ground for which they had fought so ferociously. The use of the US, British and Canadian paratroopers – essentially lightly equipped assault troops – to hold ground in Normandy against prolonged enemy attacks was a controversial distortion of

England, late May 1944: two senior NCOs of 1 Cdn Para Bn dressed in full airborne Battle Order prepare to leave Carter Barracks, Bulford, for the D-Day transit camp. They, and the warrant officer class II in the middle, all wear the battalion's gold-yellow shoulder-strap loops. The left sleeve of the WO's BD blouse seems to display the title '1/ CANADIAN PARACHUTE/ BATTALION', above the pale-blue-on-maroon 'Pegasus' patch of British Airborne Forces, above the straight pale-blue-on-maroon title 'AIRBORNE'.
(Photographer Sgt E.R.Bonter, LAC, E002852749)

March 1945: a young Canadian paratrooper cleans his 9mm Browning semi-automatic pistol during a pause in the advance into Germany. Note that his Denison smock has been modified with the addition of an upper sleeve pocket, and loops of string stitched to the shoulder areas, for securing foliage and other camouflage material. (Photographer Lt Charlie H.Richer, LAC, PA-114595)

their proper role; but despite heavy losses, 1 Cdn Para Bn held off all German counter-attacks until the eventual Allied break-out.

By the middle of August 1944 the tide had finally turned in the Normandy *bocage* country, where the British divisions had held the great majority of the German armour while the US beachhead expanded and created the conditions for the break-out. As part of 3 Para Bde, 1 Cdn Para Bn was back on the offensive for the first time since the Normandy drop. Beginning on 16 August, and continuing for the next ten days, the unit participated in an advance and a series of attacks against the German rearguard, until it was finally pulled out of the line to prepare for planned future airborne operations. On 4 September 1944, 1 Cdn Para Bn began its departure from France, and returned to its adopted home at Bulford Camp three days later. The battalion had unquestionably distinguished itself in its first campaign, though at great cost. During the three-month period between 6 June and 6 September 1944, of the original 547 paratroops who dropped on D-Day, 83 were killed, 187 were wounded and 87 became prisoners of war – a casualty rate of 65 per cent.

The Ardennes and Holland

The unit's return to England provided the opportunity to reconstitute itself. The battalion's first priority was bringing itself back up to strength, through the integration of reinforcements from 1 Cdn Para Training Company. A new commanding officer, LtCol J.A.Nicklin, replaced LtCol Bradbrooke, who had been transferred to a staff position in the Canadian Military Headquarters in London. Colonel Nicklin focused on correcting the deficiencies and shortcomings experienced during the Normandy campaign, specifically those skills required for offensive operations. As a result, a new training plan emphasized not only the basics of weapons handling and physical fitness, but also the rapid clearance of drop zones, the efficient execution of offensive and defensive battle drills, and – especially – street fighting.

However, enemy action cut this training short. Although the tide of the war had turned, the Germans, as always, proved to be a capable and energetic foe. In mid–December 1944 they launched their surprise attack in the quiet Ardennes sector, opening the campaign commonly known as the Battle of the Bulge. In the face of initial German successes that threatened to menace vital rear areas and port facilities, Allied commanders had to cobble all available forces together. As a result, on Christmas Day 1944 elements of 6th Airborne Division, including 1 Cdn

Para Bn, sailed for Ostende, Belgium. The battalion was deployed to a series of villages, where it was required to prepare defensive positions and conduct active patrolling. Although engagements with the enemy were limited to minor encounters, 1 Cdn Para Bn earned the distinction of having been the only Canadian combat unit to see action in the Ardennes.

Once the immediate crisis was over and the German columns had been first halted, and then driven back in ruin, 1 Cdn Para Bn was redeployed to Holland. By 22 January 1945, in bitter weather and in miserable terrain conditions, the unit had established a series of defensive positions on the west bank of the River Maas. Here they faced German troops manning a network of well-fortified defensive positions – part of the Siegfried Line – on the opposite bank. Over the span of the next two weeks, aggressive patrolling to test the enemy's defences ensured daily firefights and shelling. The battalion's routine continued in this vane until it was eventually relieved in mid-February 1944 by American forces. The unit's second excursion into continental Europe did not involve any major engagements, and casualties were only three killed and nine wounded due to enemy action and accidents. Importantly, however, this deployment still provided an excellent opportunity for the reconstituted battalion to settle down, allowing the reinforcements to prove themselves to the veterans. On 25 February 1945 the Canadian paratroopers returned to Carter Barracks.

The Rhine crossings
Back in Britain, the unit began to prepare for what would turn out to be their final mission. It is always a significant indicator of action ahead when a battalion is meticulously brought up to full strength and a tough training schedule is re-established. However, its duration was very short: on 19 March 1945 the paratroopers were confined to barracks. The air became heavy with anticipation, and morale was exceptionally high. Preparations for action were obviously in their final stages.

The Allies were now ready to pierce the Reich itself, crossing the historic barrier of the River Rhine. The airborne component of the mission was codenamed Operation 'Varsity'; this would involve airborne assaults by the British 6th and US 17th Airborne Divisions, approximately 5 miles north and north-west of the town of Wesel. The paratroopers would once again be dropped behind enemy lines to seize vital ground, hinder enemy reinforcements and disrupt the German lines of communications. However, this time the drop would not precede the main assault, but follow it. Senior military planners believed that greater use of firepower in support of the ground assault across the Rhine could be made if the artillery and tactical aircraft were not impeded by paratroopers dropping in the target area. The necessity for accurate insertion on to the drop zones also led commanders to decide on a daytime jump. The lessons of Normandy, and of the failure of the British 1st Airborne Division's operation at Arnhem in September 1944, were in everyone's mind.

Within the overall framework of 'Varsity', 3rd Parachute Brigade was assigned the task of seizing and clearing the 'Schnappenburg feature' and the surrounding Diersfordter Forest. Once again, Brig Hill stressed the importance of speed and initiative on the part of all ranks; he directed that 'risks will be taken, and the enemy will be attacked and destroyed wherever he is found'. The Canadian battalion was given the task of seizing the Hingendahlshof Farm on the western edge of the DZ, and capturing the village of Bergerfurth to the south of the drop zone. The battalion was thus responsible for securing the central area of the brigade's front, encompassing wooded areas near a road linking Wesel to Emmerich.

The drama began to unfold in the early evening of 23 March 1945, when the battalion's personnel emplaned in 35 C-47 Dakotas. Shortly before 1000 hours the following morning the first of 14,000 troops, delivered by a total of 1,700 aircraft and 1,300 gliders, pierced the frontier of the Reich. The brigade, consisting of 2,200 men, dropped in a span of only six minutes, with incredible accuracy, in a clearing measuring only 1,000 by 800 yards.

The Canadians jumped at 0955 hours and were immediately met by stiff resistance. The entrenched Germans had recognized the clearing as a potential drop zone, and poured fire into the assaulting paratroopers. Despite this opposition, within 35 minutes of the drop, 85 per cent of 3 Para Bde had reported in; and 1 Cdn Para Bn secured its objectives by 1130hrs, less than two hours from the time the green lights went on beside the open doors of their Dakotas.

The battalion now dug in and repelled numerous counter-attacks. Soon the issue of greatest concern was the large number of German prisoners that they had captured, who at one point equalled the strength of the battalion. This quickly became a logistical problem, since space for the confinement of prisoners was scarce and men to guard them were at a premium. Luckily, that evening the lead reconnaissance elements of the British 15th (Scottish) Division moved through the battalion to continue the advance into Germany. In the aftermath of the battle, the cost was once again tallied: of the 475 paratroopers who had jumped, approximately 67 became casualties – and among the dead was the unit's commanding officer, LtCol Jeff Nicklin. As a result, Maj Fraser Eadie took command. It was in this action that Cpl Frederick Topham, a unit medic, won the Victoria Cross for his incredible courage in rescuing a number of casualties from the fire-swept drop zone.

The collapse of the Reich
It was now clear that the end could only be weeks away, but if anything this increased the stress on the advancing Allied troops, who still faced unpredictable pockets of fierce resistance. For 1 Cdn Para Bn the final advance through north-west Germany began on 26 March 1945. Field-Marshal Montgomery issued a simple directive that set the pace of subsequent events: 'This is the time to take risks and to go "flat out"', he declared; 'if we reach the Elbe quickly, we win the war'. Prime Minister Churchill was even more forthright; haunted by the concessions granted to Stalin's Soviet Union at the Yalta Conference, he personally directed that the British forces beat the Russians to the coast of the Baltic Sea.

What followed was an aggressive six-week, 300-mile dash – advancing by day, rotating the lead units by leapfrogging battalions within the brigade, and digging in at night. The battalion marched, used wheeled transport, and rode on tanks during its push to the Baltic. The advance was punctuated by repeated and often vicious running battles with German rear-guards. However, on 2 May 1945 the battalion, as the lead element of 6th Airborne Division, entered Wismar on the Baltic Sea; and later that same day they met the advancing Red Army – the only Canadians to do so.

The war was officially declared over on 8 May 1945. Later that month the Canadian paratroopers returned to Bulford and settled impatiently into Carter Barracks once more to await their future. By chance, space was available on the liner *Isle de France;* and 1 Cdn Para Bn embarked for Canada as early as 31 May 1945. The

battalion arrived in Halifax on 21 June, the first complete Canadian unit to be repatriated. Following a parade, the paratroopers were given 30 days' leave, and they dispersed to their various parts of the country.

The battalion's personnel re-assembled at Camp Niagara-on-the-Lake, Ontario, in late July; but they returned to a unit that NDHQ had already determined was to be struck from the order of battle. It remained a unit on the War Establishment only as an administrative tool, and one with a very short life span. Sadly, on 30 September 1945, the 1st Canadian Parachute Battalion was officially disbanded.

The nation's first airborne soldiers had earned a proud and remarkable reputation. Their legacy would become the standard of excellence that would challenge Canada's future paratroopers and imbue them with a special pride. The battalion had never failed to complete an assigned mission, nor did it ever lose or surrender an objective once taken. The Canadian paratroopers were among the very first Allied soldiers to land in Occupied Europe; were the only Canadians who participated in the Battle of the Bulge; and by the end of the war, had advanced deeper into Germany than any other Canadian unit. Unquestionably, the soldiers of the 1st Canadian Parachute Battalion – as well as their supporting airborne organizations, the 1st Canadian Parachute Training Company/Battalion and A-35 Canadian Parachute Training Centre – had established, at great cost and personal sacrifice, a solid foundation of Canadian airborne experience.

POST-WAR DEVELOPMENTS

With the end of World War II priorities quickly changed. The long and costly global struggle had taken its toll, and a debt-ridden and war-weary Canadian government was intent on creating a post-war army that was anything but extravagant. Notwithstanding the military's achievements during the war, the government articulated two clear requirements for its peacetime army: firstly, it was to consist of a representative group of all arms of the service; and secondly, its primary purpose was to provide a small but highly trained and skilled professional force, that in time of conflict could expand and train the citizen soldiers who would fight that war. Within this framework, paratroopers were held to have limited relevance.

In the austere climate of 'minimum peacetime obligations', the fate of Canada's paratroopers seemed sealed. The training of new paratroopers at the Shilo centre had already ceased in May 1945. With no paratroop unit in the order of battle the need for the school seemed marginal at best; nonetheless, it remained open pending the final decisions on the structure of the post-war Army. As always, individual initiative made the difference. While they were waiting for the axe to fall the parachute school worked hard to keep abreast of airborne developments, and attempted to perpetuate the links with British and American airborne units that had been established through shared experience during the war. The efforts of the centre's commanding officer were instrumental in maintaining a degree of airborne expertise; he selectively sifted the ranks of the disbanded 1 Cdn Para Bn, and from the pool of personnel who had decided to remain in the Active Force he chose the best to act as instructors and staff for his training establishment.

Lacking any direction from Army Head-quarters, the commanding officer and his staff worked on, and these prescient efforts were soon rewarded. Their perpetuation of links with Canada's closest allies, and their staying abreast of the latest tactical developments – specifically air-transportability – provided the breath of life that airborne advocates were looking for. Not surprisingly, Canadian commanders were looking abroad for the way ahead. In 1947 a study revealed that British peacetime policy was based on training and equipping all infantry formations to be air-transportable. Discussions quickly ascertained that both the British and Americans would welcome an airborne establishment in Canada that would be capable of filling in the gaps in their knowledge – specifically, in areas such as the problem of standardization of equipment between Britain and the United States, and the need for experimental research into cold-weather conditions. To its allies Canada was the ideal intermediary.

Sgts H.C.Cook and W.W.Judd after their return from a rescue mission in the Canadian Arctic; these signallers parachuted into Moffet Inlet on 3 October 1947. They wear Inuit garments, which were superior to issue winter wear. The value of military parachutists for providing relief in various civil emergency situations was stressed by those who were fighting to retain even a limited airborne capability in the Canadian Army in the early post-war years. (Photographer Capt Dubervill, LAC, PA-189547)

Canadian military leaders quickly realized that co-operation with their closest defence partners would allow the country to benefit from an exchange of information on the latest developments and doctrine. For the airborne advocates, a test facility was not a parachute unit, but it would at least keep skills alive and allow the Canadian military to stay in the game. In the end, for the sake of efficiency of manpower and resources, NDHQ directed that the parachute training and research functions reside in a single Canadian Joint Army/Air Training Centre. As a result, on 15 August 1947 the Joint Air School (JAS) was established in Rivers, Manitoba.

For the airborne advocates the JAS became the 'foot in the door' that allowed the retention of skills required for airborne operations, for both the Army and the Royal Canadian Air Force. The school's mandate included:

(a) Research in air-portability of Army personnel and equipment.

(b) User trials of equipment, especially under cold weather conditions.

(c) Limited development and assessment of airborne equipment.

(d) Training of paratroop volunteers; training in air-portability of personnel and equipment; training in maintenance; advanced training of glider pilots in exercises with troops; training in some of the uses of light aircraft.

More importantly, the JAS – which was renamed the Canadian Joint Air Training Centre (CJATC) on 1 April 1949 – provided the seed from which airborne organizations could grow.

During its short existence in 1948, one of the Canadian SAS Company's tasks was to develop and test operational airborne uniforms and equipment. Here, two paratroopers wearing reinforced trousers with leather kneepads are ready to do battle with the Wind Machine – designed to train paratroopers to collapse their parachute canopies quickly after landing in heavy winds.
(Authors' collection)

CANADIAN SPECIAL AIR SERVICE COMPANY, 1948

The hidden agenda of the airborne advocates quickly took root. Once the permanent structure of the Army was established in 1947, they soon pushed to expand the airborne capability within the JAS by submitting a proposal that spring for a Canadian Special Air Service (SAS) Company. This new organization was to be an integral sub-unit of the Army component of the JAS, with a mandate of filling Army, inter-service, and public duties such as army/air tactical research and development; demonstrations to assist with army/air training; airborne firefighting; search and rescue; and aid to the civil power. Its development, however, proved to be quite different, as its name implies.

The initial proposal for the special sub-unit prescribed a clearly defined role. The Army, which sponsored the establishment of the fledgling organization, portrayed the SAS Company's inherent mobility as a definite asset. A military appreciation written by its proponents argued the need for the unit in terms of its potential benefit to the public. It explained that the specially trained company would provide an 'efficient life- and property-saving organization capable of moving from its base to any point in Canada in ten to fifteen hours'. Furthermore, the Canadian SAS Company was framed as critical in working in support of the RCAF air search-and-rescue duties required by the International Civil Aviation Organization agreement.

The proposed training plan further supported this benevolent image. The training cycle consisted of four phases broken down as follows: (1) Tactical Research & Development (parachute-related work and fieldcraft skills); (2) Airborne Firefighting; (3) Air Search & Rescue; and (4) Mobile Aid to the Civil Power (crowd control, first aid, military law). Conspicuously absent was any hint of the commando or specialist training which the organization's name innately implied by reference to the commando role of the British wartime Special Air Service.

In September 1947 the request for approval for the sub-unit was forwarded to the Deputy Chief of the General Staff. Significantly, it now had two additional roles added to it: public service in the event of a national catastrophe; and provision of a nucleus for expansion into parachute battalions. However, the proposal also noted that the SAS Company was required to provide the manpower for the large programme of test and development that was under way by the CJATC Tactical Research & Development Wing, as well as teams for all demonstrations within and outside the CJATC.

As support for the proposed company grew, its real identity came into sharper focus. An assessment of potential benefits to the Army included its ability to 'keep the techniques employed by [British] SAS persons during the war alive in the peacetime army.' Although this item was last in the order of priority in the list, it soon moved to the forefront.

NDHQ authorized the sub-unit with an effective date of 9 January 1948, and as soon as this was announced a dramatic change in focus became evident. Not only did the company's function as a base for expansion for the development of airborne units take precedence, but the previously subtle reference to a war-fighting, specifically special forces role also leapt into the foreground. The new Terms of Reference for the employment of the SAS Company, which was confirmed in April, outlined the following duties in a revised priority:

(a) Provide a tactical parachute company for airborne training. This company is to form the nucleus for expansion for the training of the three infantry battalions as parachute battalions;

(b) Provide a formed body of troops to participate in tactical exercises and demonstrations for courses at the CJATC and service units throughout the country.

(c) Preserve and advance the techniques of SAS [commando] operations developed during World War II.

A paratrooper of the Cdn SAS Coy collapsing a parachute canopy at Rivers, Manitoba. (Authors' collection)

(d) Provide when required parachutists to back up the RCAF organizations as detailed in the Interim Plan for Air Search & Rescue.

(e) Aid Civil Authorities in fighting forest fires and assisting in national catastrophes when authorized by Defence Headquarters.

This shift in emphasis was anything but subtle. The original stress upon aid to the civil authority and public service duties – in a soothing presentation calculated to appeal to a war-weary and fiscally anxious government – was now down-graded, if not totally marginalized. However, the Terms of Reference certainly represented a legitimate initial reaction by the Army to the government's announcement in 1946, that airborne training for the Active Force Brigade Group (i.e. the new regular army) was contemplated, and that an establishment to this end was being created.

Organization

The new organization was established at company strength – 125 all ranks. It comprised one platoon from each of the Army's three regular infantry regiments – the Royal Canadian Regiment (RCR), Royal 22nd Regiment (R22eR) and Princess Patricia's Canadian Light Infantry (PPCLI). All personnel were volunteers, most of them with wartime airborne experience, who were carefully selected. Every one of them had to be unmarried, in superb physical condition, and to demonstrate initiative, self-reliance, self-discipline, mental agility and an original approach. Captain Guy D'Artois, a wartime member of the FSSF and later of the Special Operations Executive (SOE), was posted to the company as its second-in-command, but due to a difficulty in finding a qualified major he became the acting officer commanding.

D'Artois trained his carefully selected paratroopers as a specialized commando force. His intractable approach and trademark persistence quickly made him the 'absolute despair of the senior officers at Rivers [CJATC]'. Veterans of the SAS Company explained that 'Captain D'Artois didn't understand "no". He carried on with his training regardless of what others said... Guy answered to no one, he was his own man who ran his own show'.

To date, the continued survival of the JAS and its limited airborne capability, as represented by the Canadian SAS Coy, was largely due to a British and American preoccupation with airborne and air-transportable forces in the post-war period. This was based on a concept of security established on smaller standing forces with greater tactical and strategic mobility. In essence, possession of

Parachute instructors at the Joint Air School (JAS), Rivers, Manitoba, and Cdn SAS Coy officers and NCOs. Due to equipment shortages, instructors and candidates were forced to make do with various types of American and British jump training equipment and uniforms. (Courtesy 1st Cdn Para Bn Assoc Archives)

paratroopers represented the nation's 'ready sword'. This was critical in light of the looming 1946 Canada/US Basic Security Plan (BSP), which imposed on Canada the requirement to provide one airborne/air-transportable brigade, and its necessary airlift, as its share of the overall continental defence agreement. By the summer of 1948 the SAS Coy represented the sum total of Canada's operational airborne capability. Clearly, some form of action was urgently required.

As a result, the CGS directed that training for one battalion of infantry for airborne/air-transported operations be completed by 1 April 1949. The BSP dictated that by 1 May 1949 the Canadian government be capable of deploying a battalion combat team prepared to respond immediately to any actual Soviet lodgement in the Arctic, with a second battalion available within two months, and an entire brigade group within four months. There was still a great deal to be done before Canada could possibly claim to be making realistic progress along this ambitious path.

Mobile Striking Force paratroopers of Princess Patricia's Canadian Light Infantry *en route* to their objective at Fort St John Airfield during Exercise 'Eagle', 6–7 August 1949. With the rapid conversion of three infantry battalions to an airborne role, paratroopers had to continue wearing World War II British airborne helmets, post-war British Denison smocks, Canadian Khaki Drill (Bush) uniforms, and even waterproofed rubber boots, until specialized airborne clothing and equipment was designed and purchased. Paratroopers used the American-manufactured T-10 parachutes, which were sometimes packed in T-7A carriers. (Courtesy LAC, PA-179779)

MOBILE STRIKING FORCE, 1949

The Canadian Army was now finally moving towards its airborne/air-transportable Active Brigade Group, which was titled the Mobile Striking Force (MSF). The effect of this directive was to simply swallow up the short-lived Canadian SAS Company. The highly trained SAS platoons provided the training staffs for the detachments from each of the Regular Force infantry regiments (RCR, R22eR, PPCLI) that rotated through the JAS for parachute qualification, and upon completion returned to their parent regiments to provide an experienced airborne cadre for each. The slow dissolution of the Canadian SAS Coy was formalized by the CGS when he announced that the sub-unit would not be reconstituted upon the completion of airborne conversion training by the R22eR, which was the last of the three Active Force infantry regiments to undertake it. The actual disbandment of the company was so low key that no official date exists; its personnel just melted away. Nonetheless, the SAS Coy had served a critical function in Canadian airborne history: it was the bridge that linked 1 Cdn Para Bn and the three infantry battalions that – conceptually, at least – formed an airborne brigade. In so doing, the Cdn SAS Coy perpetuated the airborne spirit and kept the requisite parachute skills alive.

The expansion of Canada's airborne capability, however, did not represent a wholesale change in philosophy by the military or political leadership in regard to airborne forces. The MSF's existence reflected the lethargy and hesitancy that went into its implementation: it was to represent a political expedient rather than a hard, operational capability. From its inception the MSF encountered a series of never-ending obstacles. Quite frankly, Canadian politicians and military commanders were never convinced that the Soviets would, or even could, launch large-scale ground operations in the Arctic. As a result, with a limited defence budget, there were no immediate funds available to provide the new parachute force with the required air transport and specialized equipment. It is therefore no surprise that practical support for an operational concept which was not considered credible by the military and political leadership remained minimal.

Implementation

The MSF's questionable status was evident from the very beginning. A test exercise, Exercise 'Eagle', was conducted in August 1949 to assess the operational efficiency of the newly converted PPCLI battalion. The scenario depicted the airborne deployment of a small, lightly armed 'Russian' force, landing and capturing the Fort St John Airfield and the Peace River Bridge in British Columbia. The 'Patricias', as part of a larger joint Canadian/US task force, were directed to destroy the enemy lodgement – specifically, to conduct a parachute assault to seize the airstrip at Fort St John Airfield, and to support the air-landing of the remainder of the battalion. Success was not achieved. The parachute drop on to the intended DZ was poorly executed; paratroopers were widely dispersed, most of them missing the target. In addition, the 'enemy's' ability to gain and maintain air superiority further reduced

PPCLI paratroopers dressed in RCAF winter flight suits, toques, winter gloves, and waterproofed winter boots, and carrying their rifle valises, undergo final jumpmaster checks prior to boarding aircraft for a winter warfare exercise. Compare with Plate C2. (Courtesy PPCLI Regimental Archives)

the effectiveness of the paratroopers. Post-exercise reports also revealed that the paratroopers were not properly equipped, and had to borrow para-chutes and other pieces of equip-ment from the CJATC (the now-renamed JAS). This exercise delivered a serious blow to the reputation of the fledgling MSF.

The government, and particularly the Minister of National Defence, were severely embarrassed by this poor showing. The political opposition in Parliament, as well as the press, denounced Canada's military ill-preparedness and the government's negligence in leaving the country's North unde-fended. In reaction, the

An Airborne Signal Support Unit paratrooper in 1954, heavily loaded with communications equipment in addition to his parachutes, personal pack and weapon. At this period it was conventional for NCOs and officers to display rank insignia on their helmets. (Courtesy CAFM)

the air threat further entrenched the perception that the MSF was irrelevant and had no credible role. Both the military and scientific communities agreed that it was impossible to construct a complete defence even against the manned bomber, much less ICBMs. Therefore, the government's policy in regard to the North evolved from one of active defence to one of simple surveillance, and the great wilderness was regarded simply as 'strategic depth'. The impact was quickly felt by Canada's airborne forces.

In January 1958 the MSF was restructured and renamed the Defence of Canada Force (DCF). The reorganization involved abandoning the airborne battalion structure; in its place, each of the three regular infantry regiments established a single parachute company (this period is commonly referred to as the era of 'Jump Companies'). Once again, these companies were organized and equipped similarly to the regular infantry companies within their respective battalions with the sole exception that the personnel were parachute qualified.

This much reduced and decentralized airborne capability was now responsible for meeting the Defence of Canada mandate, specifically the response to 'enemy lodgements'. However, a widespread belief within the Army that paratroopers were not relevant in the Canadian context ensured the continuing erosion of the airborne capability, and DCF activities and training continued to suffer from conscious and deliberate neglect. The Canadian military was completely focused on NATO's mechanized battlefield in Europe, and to a lesser degree on UN operations; airborne forces were simply a drain on limited resources. By the mid to late 1960s the DCF, as represented by the three decentralized parachute companies, was merely a shell. Like the MSF before it, it never represented a genuine operational capability, but had a purely theoretical existence – that happened to allow an attempt to keep the skills of military parachuting alive in Canada. However, the turning cycles of events would bring a change in the international security environment, and would propel Canadian airborne forces back into prominence.

The Canadian Department of External Affairs became increasingly interested in UN deployments. The UN intervention in the 1956 Suez crisis, through the use of an Emergency Force, led to growing Canadian interest and involvement. The following year Lester B. Pearson – the Canadian Secretary of State for External Affairs and the originator of the Suez Emergency Force concept – publicly asserted the need for countries to earmark small forces for UN deployments, to perform such functions as securing cease-fires that had been agreed upon by belligerents. In January 1958, Canada officially designated a Stand-By Battalion for United Nations tasks; and by the early 1960s the notion of an Army rapid reaction capability was gathering momentum. The NDHQ developed a new defence policy, based on the concept of a small air-mobile army with tactical air support.

The 1964 Defence White Paper embodied a distinct new philosophy for the Canadian Forces that was rooted in using Canada's military 'to preserve peace by deterring war'. This entailed transforming the forces into a mobile force that could meet the widest range of potential overseas requirements in the quickest possible time. The MND wanted the capability of rapidly despatching forces that could contain conflicts and prevent them from escalating into more dangerous and less manageable crises.

In 1966, LtGen Jean Victor Allard, the new Commander of Force Mobile Command (FMC – i.e. the Canadian Army), described a scale of conflicts ranging from peace-keeping operations to limited and total war. He rationalized that different elements of the Army were seen as being better suited to respond to different circumstances along that spectrum. Hence, he believed that the FMC must be structured to provide an effective and capable response for the entire spectrum of conflict. He candidly confessed that the current structure was designed primarily for only the upper end of the scale, namely a total global war; and consequently, that it demonstrated great deficiencies for the lower range of activities such as peace-keeping, counter-insurgency, guerrilla and limited warfare. LtGen Allard added that the anticipated range of potential confrontations suggested that a 'significant portion of the Canadian Army Field Force must be capable of operating in limited war in any part of the world... [the Army] must be strategically mobile and possess tactical mobility suitable to the scale of conflict and appropriate to the areas of operations.' Therefore, he felt that the Army's organization required two basic types of formations and units. Firstly, light airborne/air-transportable forces were needed for the defence of the Canada/US region, for peace-keeping, for the Allied Command Europe (ACE) Mobile Force, and for small limited wars. Secondly, Canada needed heavier armoured and mechanized forces to fulfil the commitment to NATO in Europe.

THE CANADIAN AIRBORNE REGIMENT, 1968

The concept

General Allard decided to create the necessary force of paratroops and other light troops to deal with conflicts at the lower end of the spectrum. Stressing strategic mobility, he aimed to have a completely air-portable unit, with all its equipment, deployed in the designated operational theatre as quickly as 48 hours. On 12 May 1966 the Minister of National Defence announced that '[the Army] would include the establishment of an airborne regiment whose personnel and equipment could be rapidly sent to danger zones.'

For the Army Commander the new airborne regiment represented flexibility and a high order of professionalism. 'We knew that the deployment of an infantry brigade overseas could take several weeks, and even then only if it were already completely equipped and had received at least one month's thorough training... The light and rapid airborne regiment was meant to "fill the bill" between the time the government acceded to a request for intervention from outside and the arrival of the main body of troops.'

The creation of the new airborne regiment was also suggested by a staff assessment that confirmed the obvious: that 'dispersal of parachutists in small operational and training packets [i.e. DCF model] leads to a loss of overall airborne effectiveness and efficiency'; that it violated the principle of economy by duplication of facilities, and caused unnecessary disruption and inefficiency to three battalions at any one time, and 'in the long term forced unwanted organizational changes on half the infantry corps.' The findings recommended that 'every effort must be made to concentrate all airborne operational and training resources in the one unit.'

Of equal importance was LtGen Allard's emphasis on the training value of airborne units. The Army Commander clearly believed that 'this light unit is going to be very attractive to a fellow who likes to live dangerously, so all volunteers can go into it.' His creation was to be open to all three services and manned exclusively by volunteers: 'We intend to look at the individual a little more, rather than considering the unit as a large body of troops, some of whom might not be suited for the task.'

Thus, as a result of a combination of factors – a change in defence policy and focus, Army staff analysis, and Allard's own concept of modern war-fighting and the training required to prepare individuals – the idea of a distinct airborne unit was reborn. In spring 1966, Gen Allard – now Chief of the Defence Staff (CDS) – discussed the formation of what he fondly labelled the new 'airborne commando regiment'. Colonel Donald H.Rochester was appointed as the commander-designate, and given a further year to refine the concept of operations, organization and structure. The prospects seemed unlimited. 'The exciting thing about General Allard's concept', recalled Rochester, 'was that this unit was to be radically different. Except for aircraft, it was to be self-contained, with infantry, armour, artillery, engineers, signals and supporting administration... All were to be volunteers, and so well trained in their own arm or service that they could devote their time to specialist training.' His enthusiasm is hardly surprising: to command such a unit must be the dream of any professional military officer.

Jamaica, April 1972: paratroopers of the Cdn AB Regt conduct an amphibious assault landing during Exercise 'Nimrod Caper IV'; they are armed with the 9mm C1 Sterling sub-machine gun and 7.62mm FN C1A1 7.62mm rifle. General Allard's vision for the new regiment included a wide range of operational capabilities at the lower end of the spectrum of possible threats – for peace-keeping, counter-insurgency, guerrilla and limited warfare. (Courtesy CAFM)

Organization

However, externally imposed changes began early in the administrative and planning process. A centrally directed manpower reduction scaled the regiment down from the original 1,285 all ranks to 898. The infantry components of the regiment were referred to as 'battalions', but at approximately 278 personnel they were far too small for this designation, while too large to be labelled as companies. As a result, they came to be called 'commandos' (for which term in this context there was some precedent in the French airborne forces of the 1950s). After exhaustive analysis and study, Griesbach Barracks at Canadian Forces Base (CFB) Edmonton was chosen as the location of the unit, because of its excellent air facilities and abundant drop zones; its important strategic location from a global viewpoint; its proximity to training areas at Wainwright, and to mountain and ski areas; and – particularly – because the PPCLI was to move to Calgary, and the accommodation they were vacating was a custom fit.

Finally, on 8 April 1968, the Canadian Airborne Regiment (Cdn AB Regt) was officially established. It consisted of an Airborne HQ and Signal Squadron (80 personnel); two Infantry Airborne Commandos (278 each); an Airborne Field Battery (80 personnel, capable of providing two 3-gun troops of pack howitzers, or two groups of 6x 82mm mortars); an engineer Airborne Field Squadron (81 personnel); and an Airborne Service Commando (89 personnel – combat service support and administration).

Original mandate

The regiment's mandate was impressive. The Cdn AB Regt was required to be capable of performing a variety of tasks that included: the defence of Canada; the UN 'stand-by' role; peace-keeping operations; missions in connection with national disasters; Special Air Service-type missions; *coup de main* tasks in a general war setting; and responsibility for parachute training in the CF. The respective Canadian Forces Organizational Order (CFOO) stated that 'the role of the Canadian Airborne Regiment is to provide a force capable of moving quickly to meet any unexpected enemy threat or other commitment of the Canadian Armed Forces.' In short, the nation's paratroopers now became Canada's international fire-brigade.

Members of the Cdn AB Regt mortar platoon pose as if calibrating the sights during a training exercise in Cyprus, 1974. They wear American body armour vests of two patterns – apparently M-69 and M-52 – and American helmets with the Type II parachutist liner. (Courtesy CAFM)

DZ Buxton, Edmonton, Alberta, 3 July 1977: the Cdn AB Regt's final mass drop before its move to CFB Petawawa, Ontario. (Courtesy CAFM)

The regimental commander had great expectations; he told his officers and men that a great adventure lay ahead of them, and he had reason to be optimistic. The quality of the original members of the unit was incontestable. Official recruiting material stressed the superior attributes of the new genre of airborne warrior, emphasizing that the paratrooper had to be an excellent athlete, an expert with small arms and a survival specialist, that he had to be robust, courageous and capable of a high level of endurance. Not surprisingly, the Cdn AB Regt received a high percentage of the more ambitious, determined and energized individuals. They skimmed the cream of the Army, accepting only experienced officers, non-commissioned officers and soldiers. All riflemen within the commandos were required to be qualified to the rank of corporal after previous service within a regular rifle battalion. As a result, they were already competent and experienced in the basic skills of soldiering. Equally important, they were on the whole older and, normally, more mature. This allowed the regiment to direct its efforts towards specialized training such as mountain and pathfinder operations, patrolling courses, skiing, and unarmed combat.

The Cdn AB Regt quickly forged a reputation for undertaking tough, demanding and dynamic activities. It set new standards for physical fitness and training realism. Specifically, it revolutionized the manner in which the infantry conducted live fire exercises and firing ranges. In consonance with its status as a strategic force capable of global deployment, the regiment travelled throughout Canada, the United States and more exotic locations such as Jamaica to practise its lethal craft. By the early 1970s the Airborne Regiment was at its zenith; it had the status of a mini-formation, direct access to the Commander of the Army, and an increased peacetime establishment of 1,044 all ranks.

The first major organizational change occurred in June 1970, when a mechanized infantry battalion, designated 3 Mechanized Commando (3 Mech Cdo), stationed in Baden-Soellingen, Germany, was added to the Cdn AB Regt's order of battle. This odd decision had nothing to do with operational considerations and was reached basically for reasons of administrative convenience. The new unit was an RCR/PPCLI hybrid battalion born of an Army reorganization in 1969/1970. The old Army structure contained 11 infantry battalions, plus the Cdn AB Regt with two rifle commandos. The re-organization cut several Regular Force units from the order of battle, but established the three infantry regiments – RCR, R22eR and PPCLI – with three battalions each. The existence in the order of battle of the tenth, hybrid battalion required a solution which neither demanded the establishment of a new regiment, nor altered the balance between the three surviving infantry regiments. Therefore, 3 Mech Cdo became a sub-unit of the Cdn AB Regt – essentially, because there was nowhere else to put it. It was an odd fit, but not without some advantages: although a mechanized unit, and geographically separated from its parent regiment, 3 Mech Cdo did usefully represent a Canadian airborne presence in Europe, and nurtured important links with other airborne units in NATO.

OPERATIONS

The regiment's first operational test came in the fall of 1970 during the 'Separatist Crisis' in **Quebec** sparked by the activities of the Quebec Liberation Front (FLQ). On 15 October 1970 the provincial government of Quebec officially solicited the assistance of the CF in aid of the civil power, specifically to 'help the police protect the public and public buildings'. The request was received in Ottawa at 1250 hours, and within 40 minutes two aircraft carrying the lead elements of the Cdn AB Regt departed Edmonton as part of Operation 'Essay'. The regiment set

Section formation advance to contact, spring 1980. Two paratroopers carry 66mm M-72 rocket launchers. (Courtesy CAFM)

A paratrooper displays the correct side exit jump drill from a C-130 Hercules. (Courtesy CAFM)

up its temporary quarters at St Hubert Airfield with smaller detachments located around Camp Farnham, Camp Bouchard, St Sauveur and Sorel. It was organized into four rapid reaction teams, which were tasked with assisting the municipal and provincial police forces in the conduct of sweeps, raids and other internal security missions. Each quick-response element was given a specific niche. One team was codenamed 'Eagle' and assigned as the regiment's heli-borne force. Another group, 'Speed', was equipped with wheeled transport. The third team, 'Stand-By' was ready to move anywhere, anytime, anyhow; and the fourth, 'Reserve Force', was to rotate tasks with the other groups to ensure that all had adequate opportunities to rest.

The tension and sense of crisis began to dissipate by early November, and the regiment returned to Edmonton on the 17th of that month. Overall, the Canadian Forces participation in OP 'Essay' totalled approximately 10,000 personnel; it was officially terminated on 4 January 1971.

The Airborne's next operational test came nearly four years later. It began in April 1974 with the rotation of 1 Commando to the Mediterranean island of **Cyprus**, as part of the Canadian commitment to the United Nations Force in Cyprus (UNFICYP)[3]. Upon their arrival there was already considerable unrest between the majority Greek Cypriot and minority Turkish Cypriot populations; and on 15 July the pressure cooker erupted as violent fire-fights raged throughout the city of Nicosia. By noon it became apparent that the Greek Cypriot National Guard had staged a *coup d'etat* and was now in total control of Nicosia and the government. Five days later the crisis escalated immeasurably when, in the early morning, an invasion of the island was launched by the Turkish armed forces, spearheaded by paratroop drops.

The Turkish government justified its direct military intervention on the premise that it had an obligation to safeguard the lives and rights of the Turkish Cypriot minority. Turkish parachute drops and amphibious operations soon established a corridor from Nicosia in the heart of the island to Kyrenia on the coast. It later became apparent that this was only the first phase of the plan. As the onslaught progressed it became necessary to evacuate UN observation posts because of direct and indirect fire. To make matters worse, the Greek National Guard utilized UN positions to shield its own activities, particularly the firing of mortars. Despite continuing efforts by the UN forces, it proved impossible to negotiate an armistice during the first days of the invasion.

By 24 July the situation had stabilized and a cease-fire took hold, though it was not to last. However, the temporary lull enabled the deployment of the bulk of the Airborne Regiment to augment the UN Canadian contingent that included 1 Commando. The Airborne

3 See Elite 54 *United Nations Forces 1948–94*

Regiment commander, Col G.H.Lessard, subsequently assumed command on 2 August. Now that the contingent was reinforced by additional personnel and armoured personnel carriers (APCs), it began to flex its muscle and insist on freedom of movement. On numerous occasions roadblocks put up by Turkish forces and the Greek National Guard were forcibly removed. In addition, more observation posts were established and the entirety of 'No Man's Land' was heavily patrolled.

By mid-August 1974 UNFICYP was again put on heightened alert; and at dawn on 14 August the second phase of the Turkish offensive began. Both sides quickly began to deliberately target the UN forces. As a result, by 0812 hours the last of the Canadian positions was evacuated. In the next few days observation posts would be manned and evacuated as necessitated by events. Cease-fires were attempted but repeatedly failed. Throughout the offensive, the paratroopers and their vehicles were consistently targeted and engaged by both small-arms and mortar fire. Two days later, with their objectives secured, the Turks implemented a unilateral cease-fire. However, the situation remained tense as both sides settled uneasily into defensive positions.

Throughout this period a firm, resolute stand by the Canadian paratroopers maintained the integrity of the buffer zone. Despite the cessation of hostilities the environment remained dangerous. The regiment undertook the tasks of establishing and enforcing the demarcation line, providing organization and security for prisoner-of-war exchanges, and providing escorts for infrastructure repair. The Canadian troops also assisted 20,000 refugees; the paratroopers delivered tons of food and supplies, including blankets, cots and tents, prior to the arrival of the International Committee of the Red Cross (ICRC) and other humanitarian agencies.

For their efforts, the Airborne soldiers earned two Stars of Courage and six Medals of Bravery. In the brief period the regiment was engaged in this conflict, it suffered two dead and 28 wounded.

Upon the regiment's return to Canada it once again commenced its demanding training cycle. Less than two years later the Airborne found itself deployed on operations for the third time, again on home security duties. During the first week of July 1976 the regiment deployed on OP 'Gamescan', which was the designation given to the CF security operation at the 1976 **Montreal Olympics**. Given the catastrophe suffered at the Munich Olympics four years previously, significant security precautions were obviously necessary. Designated as Task Force III, the Airborne soldiers once again found themselves performing the role of a quick-reaction force. They ably demonstrated their expertise and versatility, and fortunately they were never called upon to react to a genuine crisis.

Exercise 'Lightning Strike', Goose Bay, Labrador, January 1986. During the 1980s several improvements were made to the winter uniforms: cotton was replaced with more practical waterproof nylon material, and the bulky wooden snowshoes were phased out in favour of the lighter and more durable aluminium model. (Courtesy CAFM)

REORGANIZATION: THE SPECIAL SERVICE FORCE, 1976

Had they but known it, the Canadian Airborne Regiment had reached its apex. From now on continual budgetary pressures would slowly erode the resources and strength of the Canadian Forces. In December 1974 the cabinet authorized a Defence Structure Review. General Jacques Dextraze, the CDS, quickly announced that 'hard operational needs would determine the basic structuring of the forces'. It was clear that only those organizations that had a long-term and indisputable role to fill could breathe easily; and unfortunately, the CDS perceived parachute soldiers as both costly and redundant. It was predictable that he would have supporters; in every army, elite units that cream off the best men, and are seen as enjoying priority for resources, tend to be unpopular.

Dextraze dismissed the Airborne's importance as 'protectors of the North', announcing that he did not believe that paratroops were an economical or effective tool for the task. In late December 1975 he briefed a gathering in Montreal that one of the units considered for disbandment as part of the ongoing Defence Structure Review was the Airborne Regiment. The CDS later publicly declared that he could not afford to have any one formation of the Canadian Forces become unduly specialized. Dextraze's perception of the Airborne's role was one of simply assisting every other formation, and the government, in any missions the CF might be given. He did not ascribe to them any special responsibility or status.

The initial musings about disbandment fomented a storm of resistance. As a result, Gen Dextraze deftly took a new approach. In Ottawa the following year he confided to a highly influential lobby group, the Conference of Defence Associates: 'My two major problems with the current Army posture are that it could be better balanced geographically, and that I do not have enough people to fill the sharp end vacancies which exist'. Dextraze then opined that he could correct these problems by relocating the Cdn AB Regt and subordinating it to another formation. He explained that the Army would then have three, rather than four major formations in Canada, each with integral supporting arms and services.

CFB Petawawa, August 1987: MajGen Kent R.Foster wears the Canadian Forces' new summer Service Dress, Tan, Distinctive Environmental Uniform (DEU) while inspecting Cdn AB Regt personnel. The paratroopers are wearing CF Rifle Green DEU uniforms and distinctive high-laced SSF parade boots. Compare this photograph with Plates E3 and F3. (Courtesy CAFM)

(continued on page 41)

1ST CANADIAN PARACHUTE BATTALION
1: Captain, service dress; Canada, 1942–45
2: Parachute candidate; Ft Benning, GA, 1942–43
3: Private; Camp Shilo, Manitoba, 1943

1

2

3

A

1ST CANADIAN PARACHUTE BATTALION
1: Private; North-West Europe, 1944–45
2: Private, Op 'Varsity'; Germany, 1945
3: CQSM, Germany, 1945

B

CANADIAN SAS COMPANY & MOBILE STRIKING FORCE
1: Private, PPCLI Platoon, Cdn SAS Coy; Rivers, Manitoba, 1948
2: Sergeant, R22eR, MSF; Rivers, 1950s
3: Private, PPCLI, MSF; Rivers, 1950s

MOBILE STRIKING FORCE & DEFENCE OF CANADA FORCE
1: Private, RCR, MSF; Camp Petawawa, Ontario, 1950s
2: Private, RCR, MSF; Toronto, Ontario, 1951
3: Sergeant jump master, CJATC; Rivers, Manitoba, 1956

CANADIAN AIRBORNE REGIMENT
1: Warrant Officer; UNFICYP, Cyprus, 1974
2: Corporal; CFB Petawawa, late 1970s
3: Sergeant, service dress, 1968–86

CANADIAN AIRBORNE REGIMENT
1: Pathfinder; CFB Petawawa, 1980s
2: LMG gunner; UNITAF, Somalia, 1993
3: Major, summer service dress; CFB Petawawa, 1994

2

3

1

PARACHUTE COMPANIES
1: Corporal, Para Coy, 3rd Bn RCR-LI; CFB Petawawa, winter 1996
2: Sergeant, Para Coy, 3rd Bn R22eR-LI; East Timor, 1999
3: Corporal, Para Coy, 3rd Bn RCR-LI; Afghanistan, 2003

3

2

1

13

1

7

14

2

8

16

3

9

1
CANADIAN PARACHUTE
BATTALION

9
CANADA

16
OSONS

15

4
AIRBORNE
CANADA

10
CANADA

11

5

6

12

17

H

General Dextraze also visualized the establishment of a highly mobile, rapid reaction formation stationed in the centre of Canada, with its headquarters in CFB Petawawa. The CDS outlined that the organization would consist of an air-landed battalion, and a major airborne unit formed from the current Cdn AB Regt in which there would be a commando each from the RCR, PPCLI and R22eR. Dextraze subsequently ordered the preparation of a plan for the reorganization and relocation of the Army in Canada along these lines.

On 26 November 1976 the decision to move the Cdn AB Regt to Petawawa was formally authorized by the cabinet. Dextraze had achieved his goal: he now had a peacetime establishment based on a standard brigade group in the West, a standard brigade group in the East, and a force of regimental size in the Centre, which he tentatively designated the 'Special Service Force' (SSF). This should provide the Army with a relatively light, airborne/air-portable quick-reaction force in the demographic centre of the country, which could be moved quickly to augment either of the flanking brigades for internal security tasks, to the Arctic, or to UN-type operations.

However, the move and reorganization became a defining moment for the Cdn AB Regt, signalling nothing short of the organization's eventual demise. Of prime importance, and instrumental to the regiment's subsequent decline, was the loss of independent formation status; it was now simply an integral part of the newly created SSF. The Cdn AB Regt became nothing more than just another infantry unit, albeit an airborne one. It lost its special exemption from some tasks, and was now given assignments in the same manner as the other units within the SSF. However, there was a more serious consequence. As the regiment became defined and viewed as just another infantry unit, its claim on seasoned officers and soldiers was dismissed. Tragically, it lost its preferred standards of manning, and was no longer in the enviable position of receiving only experienced and mature leaders and men. After the move to CFB Petawawa, the former requirement that all soldiers be qualified to the level of corporal was no longer enforced. The resultant influx of younger, immature and junior soldiers had an eventual

Cyprus, 1986: HRH Prince Charles, as Colonel of Britain's Parachute Regiment, chats to Cdn AB Regt paratroopers; during this tour the two regiments became officially affiliated. Prince Charles wears a post-war Denison smock; the colonel's rank on his shoulder straps marks his honorary status, but the jump wings were earned. The paratrooper at right displays the Special Service Force sleeve patch. (Courtesy CAFM)

Airborne gunners from 'E' Battery, 2 Royal Canadian Horse Artillery rigged for a winter exercise jump on 21 January 1989. This sub-unit was assigned to provide the Cdn AB Regt with artillery support after the regiment lost its integral artillery component. (Courtesy CAFM)

impact on the character and reputation of the Canadian Airborne.

The restructuring inflicted additional wounds. The regiment was dramatically pared down, losing its integral airborne engineer squadron and artillery battery. The requirement to fulfil those capabilities fell to 2 Combat Engineer Regt and E Bty, 2 Royal Canadian Horse Artillery, within the SSF, which were responsible for providing airborne-qualified personnel and equipment in support of the Cdn AB Regt when required. The regiment, when so configured, became designated as the Cdn AB Regt Battle Group (Cdn AB Regt BG). In addition, the Airborne Service Support Unit was also disbanded. First-line service support was provided by the newly formed 1 AB Service Support Coy, and second-line support by 2 Service Bn, which was another unit within the SSF. Also stricken from the order of battle was 3 Mech Cdo; that unit's personnel were returned to Canada, and subsequently re-badged to form 3 RCR, which was newly established in CFB Petawawa.

As part of the reorganization a third rifle commando, designated 3 AB Cdo, was authorized, but not yet organized or manned. Despite the reduction in size, the reorganization entailed the addition of two new tasks. The first was to provide a quick-response airborne capability as part of the national rescue plan in the event of a major air disaster (MAJAID). The second was the necessity for the regiment to be capable of acting as a Cyprus commitment rotation unit.

In June 1979, 3 AB Cdo was officially established as the third rifle commando within the Cdn AB Regt; the regiment's infantry units were now organized so that each of the three commandos became affiliated with their parent infantry regiment – 1, 2, and 3 AB Cdos were manned by officers and men of the R22eR, PPCLI and RCR respectively. The senior Army leadership believed that this initiative would solve the regiment's chronic manpower shortages; each parent infantry regiment had a quota to fill to meet the requirements of its respective commando, so any shortfalls would be highly visible and easily attributable to the source. It was also argued that affiliating commandos to a specific 'feeder' infantry regiment would ensure that, as a matter of pride, these regiments would send only their best personnel to the Airborne Regiment. The contradiction between these two beliefs is evident to any experienced observer.

Nonetheless, with the commencement of the 1980s, Edmonton had become a memory and the paratroopers settled into their new home. In 1981 the regiment returned to Cyprus, this time under more tranquil circumstances, as the 35th Canadian peace-keeping rotation to UNFICYP; the tour was routine and uneventful. Upon the Airborne soldiers' return to Canada they resumed their trademark pace of challenging training.

Militia augmentation

In the spring of 1983 the regiment reaped a windfall as a result of a programme under which Militia units were tasked to provide integral, operationally ready sub-units for the defence of Canada. Consequently, the Cdn AB Regt became distinctly linked to three Militia regiments: Le Régiment du Saguenay (R du Sag), the Loyal Edmonton Regiment (L Edmn R), and the Queen's Own Rifles of Canada (QOR of C). Each of these Militia units was tasked by FMC with the responsibility of providing an airborne platoon to augment 1, 2 & 3 AB Cdos respectively with trained parachutists, for reinforcement in the case of an emergency. Two years later the airborne tasking was expanded; the Royal Westminster Regiment (R Westmr R) was now added to the family, becoming responsible for supplying, on order, an airborne platoon to reinforce 2 AB Commando. In addition, the existing tasking to the other Militia units was also enlarged.

The 'Total Force' concept now provided a potentially significant addition to the Airborne. The Militia augmentation represented a total of two operationally tasked company headquarters (QOR of C, and R du Sag), and six platoons broken down as follows: two from QOR of C, two from R du Sag, one from L Edmn R, and one from Royal Westminster Regiment. It was now possible, in times of crisis, that three of the Militia platoons could form the fourth platoon of each of the Airborne Regiment's rifle commandos. Furthermore, the remaining Militia platoons and a composite Militia company headquarters could also form the nucleus of a fourth commando.

Throughout the 1980s the rapid pace of Airborne soldiering continued. The Cdn AB Regt continued to focus its efforts on the UN Ready Force and Defence of Canada (DCO) roles. Major activities included Exercise 'Nimrod Caper' in Fort Bliss, Texas, in 1985. This deployment was designed to rehearse the Cdn AB Regt Battle Group, as the UN Immediate Reaction Force, for deployment and stability operations within a UN context. During this period the regiment was also heavily involved in the SSF-controlled Exercise 'Lightning Strike' series that focused on the DCO role.

In addition, the regiment was also called upon to conduct another UNFICYP rotation in the fall of 1986. Although the tour was uneventful, the regiment did take the opportunity to maximize its proximity to the British Parachute Regiment, which also had a battalion serving in Cyprus; unit exchanges and joint training were undertaken. Before the end of the tour the two regiments became officially affiliated.

A paratrooper with 1964-pattern webbing equipment in full Marching Order, photographed during one of the Cdn AB Regt's famously gruelling forced marches. (Courtesy CAFM)

In 1990/1991 the regiment assisted in the preparations to deploy communication and service support units to Iran/Iraq and Namibia, as well as to provide support to 1 RCR and 2 Field Ambulance as they deployed to the Gulf War. In addition, they trained for potential deployment for another internal security operation. On 17 August 1990, after a month long stand-off between Mohawk Natives and law enforcement officers, the **Quebec** government asked the CF to replace the provincial police at the barricades of Oka. Ten days later the provincial government submitted a further request to dismantle the Mohawk barriers. Elements of both the SSF and 5 Cdn Mech Bde Gp were swiftly deployed, and the Army Commander also ordered the Cdn AB Regt to prepare for possible deployment to Oka – the paratroopers were his 'ace in the hole'. As a result, six weeks of diligent training were undertaken; mock-ups of the barricades were constructed, and the paratroopers exercised every conceivable contingency. However, the crisis ended on 26 September without the necessity of deploying the regiment.

In mid-July 1991 the MND announced that Canada was contributing 740 troops to participate in the UN mission to allow a referendum to be held on the future of the **Western Sahara**, which was disputed between Morocco and the local Polisario movement. Of primary significance was the fact that the contribution for the new mission, designated OP 'Python', was based on the Airborne Regiment. The paratroopers were assigned the role of monitoring a proposed cease-fire and ensuring that troop reductions and prisoner exchanges, mutually agreed by Polisario and the Royal Moroccan Army, were honoured. Training for the deployment began on 1 September, and the regiment was to be in position in the Western Sahara by the beginning of November. Unfortunately, the operation never materialized. The two warring factions failed to resolve the issue of who was qualified to vote in the referendum, and consequently the proposed UN mission collapsed. The focus of the international body now switched to simply trying to sustain the existing observers in place.

Reductions

Continuing budgetary restraints resulted in yet another reorganization being imposed on the Airborne Regiment. Concurrent with the preparations for the abortive OP 'Python' was an announcement directing its official reduction from regimental to battalion status. The new structure took effect on 24 June 1992.

The reorganization reduced the regiment from a strength of 754 down to 601 all ranks. Surprisingly, despite the reduction of strength and resources, there was no change to the unit's official role. The restructured 'airborne battalion' retained the identical role and tasks,

During the regiment's deployment to Somalia, 1992–93, additional dress items such as the commercially-made wide-brimmed 'Tilley hat' – which was dyed green – and American desert boots were issued to paratroopers in theatre. This airborne soldier, photographed during a search for weapons in an outlying village, wears the 1982-pattern webbing Fighting Order and carries a 5.56mm C7 rifle. (Courtesy E.Barry) namely, to 'provide rapid deployment airborne/air-transportable forces capable of responding to any emergency situation in support of national security or international peace-keeping'. Despite the regression to battalion status, however, the airborne unit was authorized to retain the designation Cdn AB Regt; the reason lay more in economy than concern over tradition – the significant investment in regimental accoutrements, associations, clothing, kit shops, messes and museums was not something to be cheaply tampered with. The reorganization had little effect on the rank and file. To the paratroopers within the rifle commandos little seemed to change: training remained constant, demanding and hectic. Issues relating to command ranks, legalities concerning reduced authority and powers of punishments, and the nuances of new titles were irrelevant to the soldiers and junior officers.

OPERATIONS: SOMALIA, 1992–93

Athough not discernable at the time, the summer of 1992 sparked another chain of events that would dramatically affect the fortunes of Canada's airborne soldiers. At this time, UN Security Council Resolution 767 called for the Secretary-General and the international community to provide urgent humanitarian assistance to Somalia in the Horn of Africa, where years of warfare, armed chaos and famine had reduced the population to a pitiable condition. Canada quickly offered to provide transport aircraft to deliver relief supplies; and in early September the Minister of National Defence announced the deployment of 750 peace-keepers as part of a UN peace-keeping operation mandated under Chapter VI of the UN Charter. The subsequent Canadian designation for its contribution to the UN Operation in Somalia (UNOSOM) was OP 'Cordon'.

The Canadian contingent was slated to operate out of the port of Bossasso and to share the area of the old British protectorate in northern and north-eastern Somalia in co-ordination with an Australian battalion. Its tentatively defined task was to provide security for the

Somalia, 1992–93: men of a mounted patrol from 3 Cdo, Cdn AB Regt endure the heat and dust while riding a 'Grizzly' Armoured Vehicle General Purpose (AVGP). Two 5.56mm C9 light machine guns are visible.

Hugh Tremblay, the Director of Humanitarian Relief and Rehabilitation in Somalia, held up the paratroopers as a model for others. 'If you want to know and to see what you should do while you are here in Somalia', he repeatedly told visitors, 'go to Belet Huen, talk to the Canadians, and do what they have done... Emulate the Canadians and you will have success in your humanitarian relief sector'. (Courtesy CAFM)

Belet Huen, Somalia, 1993: a Cdn AB Regt paratrooper carries in a confiscated World War II-vintage Italian 6.5mm Breda M30 machine gun. (Courtesy DND Canadian Joint Imagery Library (CJIL), ISC 93-18)

distribution of humanitarian relief, as well as participating in limited local humanitarian projects. The mission fell to the Canadian Airborne Regiment.

By mid-November the paratroopers were declared 'operationally ready'. Despite some initial concerns over transforming the airborne force from a light infantry to a mechanized role (due to the armoured personnel carriers they would be using), as well as some disciplinary and training concerns, the SSF Commander declared that the Cdn AB Regt represented the best unit Canada possessed to meet the exacting and warlike conditions of the looming Somalia mission.

Unfortunately, the mission, which was to have been launched by the end of September, had now dragged well into November, and by the end of that month events quickly unravelled. The Security Council fundamentally changed the entire scope of the mission: the new mandate, in accordance with Security Council Resolution 794, called for enforcement action under Chapter VII of the UN Charter. Almost overnight, the mission had changed from peace-keeping to the much more hazardous and difficult prospect of peace-making. The paratroopers were now responsible for imposing a peace on the antagonists, by the use of force if necessary. Accordingly, on 2 December 1992 OP 'Cordon' was suspended, and two days later it was formally cancelled.

On 5 December a new warning order was issued. The national designation for Canada's participation in the new American-led enforcement operation – the Unified Task Force (UNITAF) – was OP 'Deliverance'. The paratroopers were now part of a 'peace enforcement action to ease the suffering of the Somalian people'. Within the UNITAF mission the Canadians were specifically tasked with providing a secure environment for the distribution of supplies in the Canadian Humanitarian Relief Sector (HRS), an area covering approximately 30,000 square kilometres (11,500 square miles). This translated into ensuring the security of airports; the protection of food convoys and distribution centres; the rebuilding of infrastructure, including roads, bridges and schools; the re-establishment of a local police force in Belet Huen, and numerous other humanitarian projects.

Unfortunately, the Cdn AB Regt in UNITAF experienced disciplinary problems that distracted attention from their collective performance in Somalia. Incidents included the mistreatment of prisoners on several occasions; the alleged unjustified shooting and resultant death of an intruder; and the torture and death of an apprehended thief, Shidane Arone. Unreasonably, but inevitably, this small number of appalling events ultimately brought such notoriety down on the Airborne Regiment that its very real achievements were obliterated from the public consciousness. Individual cases of poor leadership, and the criminal actions of a few, began a process which would culminate in the Cdn AB Regt's eventual demise.

Objectively examined, the Airborne's actual contribution to the amelioration of the suffering in Somalia was extremely laudable. The paratroopers arrived in Somalia in December 1992 and January 1993 – the hottest time of the year – into conditions that were later acknowledged as being 'as extreme as Canadian troops have ever encountered'. Aside from the exhausting desert temperature, the soldiers were faced with the threat of diseases such as cholera, hepatitis, malaria, typhoid, tuberculosis and numerous others. Venomous insects and snakes were widespread, and tenacious parasites were virtually unavoidable. All local water, even when boiled, was undrinkable. To further complicate operations, the Canadian area of responsibility was home to the 'militias' – heavily armed marauding gangs – of the three most powerful faction leaders in Somalia, and also encompassed the turbulent Ethiopian border.

In spite of these formidable obstacles, the Cdn AB Regt BG actively proceeded to fulfill its mandate. Their unremitting physical presence, achieved through a combination of dialogue and military operations, soon created an atmosphere of control, dominance and security. The Airborne programme was so successful that the Belet Huen HRS was declared 'secure' by UNITAF Headquarters in a period of less than three months.

Somalia, January 1993: this Cdn AB Regt trooper wears an experimental tan combat uniform. (Photographer Sgt Snoshall, DND CJIL, ISC 93-10301)

As remarkable as the Group's pacification programme was, its humanitarian effort was even more praiseworthy. Robert Press, a correspondent for the *Christian Science Monitor*, wrote: 'Belet Huen appears to be a model in Somalia for restoring peace and effectively using foreign troops during this country's transition from anarchy to a national government'. Accolades from UN mandarins and UNITAF military commanders were equally warm. Jonathan T.Howe, the Special Representative to the UN Secretary-General, stated that 'the work of your unit [Cdn AB Regt BG] in its area of operations in both military and humanitarian aspects of the mission has been outstanding'. Robert Oakley, the American Special Envoy to Somalia, confirmed that 'there is no question but that their [Cdn AB Regt BG's] discipline, operational readiness, immediate responsiveness to assigned tasks, care and use of equipment, and ability to operate effectively in difficult climatic conditions were considered to be at the very top of all UNITAF units'. Lieutenant-General R.B.Johnston, the American UNITAF Commander, judged that 'The Canadian Airborne Regiment has performed with great distinction, and the Canadian people should view its role in this historic humanitarian mission with enormous pride'. Tribute from Canadian diplomats was at first equally generous. Barbara McDougall, the Secretary of State for External Affairs, declared that Canadian paratroopers had performed a 'modern miracle'; and the Canadian High Commissioner to Somalia, Her Excellency Lucie Edwards, said that the paratroopers 'have only added lustre to their reputation as peace-keepers'.

The Airborne's achievements included the formation of five local committees to restore local government; the conduct of approximately 60 humanitarian convoys which provided aid to 96 villages; the construction of four schools attended by 5,400 pupils; the instruction and training of 272 school teachers; the supervision and training of local doctors and nurses; the training of 185 policemen in Belet Huen, Matabaan and St Emily; the provision of potable water to local refugees, and the repair of approximately 20 wells; the repair of village generators; the repair of the Belet Huen and Matabaan hospitals; the construction of a bridge; and the repair of over 200km (124 miles) of road.

Tragically, despite their commendable achievements, the mission was redefined in the media and the public consciousness as a failure. The paratroopers collectively became outcasts; the inexplicable and lamentable torture and killing of Shidane Arone became the defining image of the Airborne's operation in Africa, and the regiment suffered from overwhelmingly negative media attention. Predictably, the regiment was placed under unprecedented examination by both military and public institutions. A number of internal and external inquiries and a series of courts-martial were all conducted under media scrutiny, ensuring that the spotlight remained focused on the ostracized paratroopers.

Fort Benning, GA, 1994: paratroopers of 3 Commando 'assault' the fortified compound at K22 Range. (Courtesy CAFM)

In the aftermath of Somalia

The Cdn AB Regt attempted to rebuild its shattered image; it was clear that words would not be enough – to re-establish its reputation meant demonstrating that the unit was the most operationally ready battalion in the CF. To assist with this process the Army Commander transferred the NATO ACE Mobile Force (Land) role to the paratroopers. This was perceived by Airborne supporters as a means of solidifying the regiment's place in the Army organization, as well as providing a rationale for restructuring the regiment with a view to increasing its manpower and equipment.

An internal reorganization, designed to improve its organic combat capability in consonance with its new task, was soon undertaken. By the end of September 1993 the Airborne's strength increased from 601 to 665 all ranks by the addition of an Air Defence Platoon and an Airborne Engineer Platoon within the Combat Support Commando. A specific mandate was introduced that was intended to provide a clear aim for the Airborne soldiers to focus on. The new mission statement defined the requirement as 'the parachute delivery of 540 personnel, 12 vehicles and over 50 tons of combat supplies, at night, from 650 feet above ground level, onto one or more Drop Zones, with the complete force on the ground in less than 10 minutes.'

Gosport, England, 4 June 1994: members of 3 Cdo, Cdn AB Regt wearing Service Dress, Tan DEU, march off parade during D-Day 50th anniversary ceremonies. (Courtesy CAFM)

The realm of the operational was not the only area of focus, and the Cdn AB Regt worked diligently in other spheres at redeeming its tattered image. In addition to a gruelling training schedule, the regiment demonstrated its prowess in the competitive arena: the paratroopers won the 1994 Canadian Forces Small Arms Competition, and provided the esteemed Queen's Medallist (top scoring individual marksman in the CF). The Airborne also won the vaunted Hamilton Gault Trophy, awarded to the infantry battalion with the highest unit aggregate score for its annual marksmanship results, as well as timings for the two mandatory 10-mile forced marches conducted on two consecutive days. Furthermore, the regimental team, representing Canada, won the prestigious North European Command Infantry Competition (NECIC), putting up the best Canadian performance in the competition's history.

Deceptively, the regiment's fortunes appeared to be improving. In the summer of 1994 the Cdn AB Regt was tasked to support two separate missions deploying to **Rwanda**, the African country torn apart by unspeakable tribal genocide. A pair of platoons were dispatched to provide the security element for both OP 'Passage', a Canadian-sponsored humanitarian mission in reaction to Rwanda's cholera epidemic, and OP 'Lance', the Canadian participation in the UN Assistance Mission in Rwanda (UNAMIR). The paratroopers once again demonstrated their worth. Reports of mass killings in the south-east region of Rwanda prompted the rapid dispatch of the Airborne platoon attached to 1 Cdn Div Signals & HQ Regt to that area, to provide a presence and to determine the truth of the rumours. Their resultant performance earned them the unstinting praise of the UNAMIR II

Commander: 'The local government and military commanders were convinced that the Canadians had deployed at least one and perhaps two companies into the sector. Most of the villages in the sector were deserted at the beginning. After constant patrolling of all villages, the people gained confidence in the level of security afforded them and started to return.' Three weeks after the commencement of the mission the exhausted paratroopers, who numbered fewer than 40, passed responsibility for the sector to an entire Nigerian infantry battalion.

Another reason for hope came on 5 January 1995, when NDHQ announced that the Cdn AB Regt was chosen to replace 1 RCR in Sector South in Croatia the following spring. The airborne soldiers were being given an opportunity to prove themselves on another operational tour. Regrettably, whether or not this attempt at salvation would have silenced the Airborne's enemies became a moot point.

Scandal and disbandment

On 15 January 1995 the CTV television network broadcast excerpts from a video made by some paratroopers during their tour in Somalia. The video clips showed several paratroopers making racial slurs and behaving in an unprofessional manner. Media and political reaction was trenchant, and the apparition of Somalia once again emerged to haunt the regiment. The stage was now set for the mortal blow, which was delivered just three days later. Another amateur video was screened, this time portraying a 1 Cdo 'initiation party' back in 1992; it showed soldiers engaged in degrading and disgusting activities, again with racist overtones.

Although strictly irrelevant to the Somalia controversy, the tape devastated what was left of the Cdn AB Regt's image. Its release not only embarrassed the government and the CF, but shocked the sensibilities of a general public who, as always, remained wilfully innocent of the rougher side of life in any army. It quickly became apparent that although this spectacle was three years in the past, it had alienated any remaining support for the regiment, and cleared the way for its destruction. The Minister of National Defence swiftly ordered an investigation, although many believed that a decision had already been reached. Ominously, shortly after the airing of the video, the Prime Minister bluntly warned, 'if we have to dismantle [the Cdn AB Regt], we'll dismantle it. I have no problem with that at all.'

The Army's report on the incident was submitted to the minister on 23 January. It stated that an objective analysis of the facts demonstrated that the current Airborne Regiment was distinctly different from the unit in Somalia, and concluded that a 'line in the sand' had truly been

Kigali, Rwanda, summer 1995: during the regiment's last overseas operational deployment, Cdn AB Regt paratroopers – wearing blue UN field caps – stand in front of a BTR 60 APC abandoned by Bangladeshi UN troops. (Courtesy CAFM)

drawn. However, during the course of the investigation the disclosure of a third video depicting yet another 1 Cdo initiation ceremony, from the summer of 1994, undermined this argument. Although the behaviour depicted in the most recent tape was not as offensive as before, the fact that this type of forbidden activity was still occurring merely confirmed latent suspicions. An official press release was scheduled for the same afternoon, at which Defence Minister David Collenette announced: 'Although our senior military officers believe the regiment as constituted should continue, the government believes it cannot. Therefore, today, under the authority of the National Defence Act, I have ordered the disbandment of the Canadian Airborne Regiment.'

The MND explained that the conduct of some members of the Airborne Regiment over the past few years denigrated the reputation of all members, past and present, and brought into question the trust others bestowed in the CF. The minister announced that the cumulative effect on the public's confidence in the regiment led him to conclude that it had to be disbanded. On the weekend of 4–5 March 1995 the elaborate and well-attended final disbandment ceremonies were conducted in CFB Petawawa. At that time the last regimental commander asserted: 'Let the message be clear. Those of us who serve the regiment today are not moving on in disgrace. We have loyally and very credibly carried the standard of soldiering excellence passed to us from those paratroopers who came before. We need not look down, but continue to hold our heads high and stare straight ahead, knowing we stood in the door and were always ready to do our duty.'

SURVIVAL OF AIRBORNE CAPABILITY

3 Commando Group

Amazingly, the consequences of the destruction of the Cdn AB Regt – the forfeiture of a capability to rapidly project national power, whether for domestic or international crises – was not immediately realized. It was only during the ensuing turmoil and confusion, a scant few days prior to the officially directed disbandment date of 5 March, that Headquarters addressed the potential dilemma. 'There are some outstanding operational tasks', declared the Army Commander, 'which an element of the regiment must be prepared to execute'. Therefore, he directed the commanding officer of the Canadian Airborne Holding Unit (Cdn AB HU) – the designation given to the remaining elements of the Cdn AB Regt as of 6 March – to develop a company-size group to provide contingency troops in the event of short-notice operations. Based primarily on RCR members, this was not to exceed 300 personnel, with appropriate command and control as well as elements of Airborne Service Commando. A detailed message from Army headquarters explained that 'Canadians will not accept the contention that we cannot put troops on the ground anywhere in this country at any time'.

As a result, a second 'airborne bridge' was formed, analogous to that created by the Canadian SAS Coy in the post-World War II era. This re-designated 3 Commando Group (3 Cdo Gp) was brought back to life with an increased authorized strength of 187 paratroopers, divided into three rifle platoons and a support weapons platoon. Its combat service support was provided by the Cdn AB Regt Holding Unit. The establishment of 3 Cdo Gp, now representing Canada's sole interim airborne capability, officially took effect on 6 March 1995.

In the span of a few short days Canada's provisional parachute force went from the brink of oblivion to a state of continual high readiness. The 3 Cdo Gp was on a perpetual footing that required it to be capable of deploying on operations within 48 hours of notification. It was specifically tasked as a vanguard to conduct territorial and continental defence operations; conduct domestic/regional tasks; conduct surveillance and reconnaissance of the Canadian landmass to demonstrate national presence; and as an Immediate Reaction Force Vanguard for domestic operations, for employment in areas where conventional forces could not be deployed in a timely fashion.

Training, which had ceased with the MND's announcement in January, now quickly returned to its former hectic pace. The focus of parachuting also returned to a strictly tactical orientation. The 3 Cdo Gp activities included demonstrations on airmobile planning and execution, as well as the conduct of a comprehensive live-fire battle school. In addition, a busy cycle of urban warfare, internal security and demolition training was capped by a demonstration of the importance and viability of airborne troops. The presentation took the form of a three-aircraft Commando Group operation designated Exercise 'Lethal Reach'. It was specifically designed to display the flexibility, speed and strategic capability of airborne forces. The paratroopers jumped into

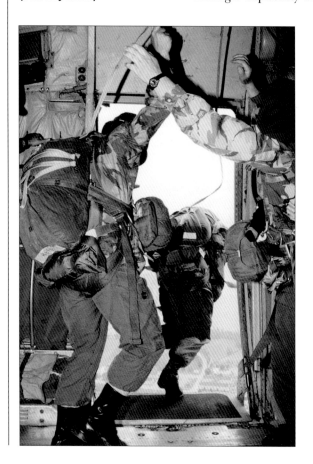

Demonstration jump by Canadian Parachute Centre personnel at Trenton, Ontario, 1997. The CPC instructors were the last Canadian paratroopers to wear the 1975-pattern camouflage jump smock. (Courtesy CAFM)

DZ Lindsay Valley, in CFB Gagetown, New Brunswick, on the night of 6 June to strike a hypothetical insurgent staging base. Despite a poor drop, the target was successfully neutralized and the paratroopers were back at their home base in CFB Petawawa in less than 36 hours. This demonstration confirmed a central tenet of airborne forces, namely the ability to reach out and influence a situation half a country away, literally in hours. In the interim, everyone waited for the government's decision on what the final form of Canada's airborne capability would be.

A return to Parachute Companies

On 12 April 1995 the Army Commander revealed that the new plan was for a decentralized capability. 'The Land Force', he explained, 'will initially maintain its parachute capability by establishing three independent Parachute Company Groups reporting to their respective Brigade Headquarters. These independent Parachute Company Groups will be the lead elements of what will eventually be three Light Infantry Battalions, to be located at CFB Edmonton, Petawawa, and Valcartier.' These light infantry battalions became based on the 3rd Bns of the three Regular Force infantry regiments (RCR, R22eR & PPCLI).

On 1 September 1995 the Cdn AB HU ceased to exist and its remaining personnel were absorbed by 3 RCR upon its move from CFB Borden to CFB Petawawa. Concomitant with this development was the transformation of 3 Cdo Gp into a new entity designated the RCR Parachute Company. It was now an integral sub-unit of 3 RCR, which in turn was one of the units chosen to become a Light Infantry Battalion (LIB). Alas, the Canadian parachute capability returned to the MSF/DCF era model. The parachute companies were organized like the battalion's other rifle companies – i.e. company HQ and three rifle platoons – with the obvious exception that all its personnel were parachute-qualified. In total, each of the three LIBs is allotted 128 parachute positions, as follows: 104 paratroopers for the Parachute Coy; 3 packer-riggers within the administrative support company; and 21 parachute positions within each LIB's reconnaissance platoon.

This decentralized organization heightened the importance of the newly designated Canadian Parachute Centre (CPC – formerly known as the Canadian Airborne Centre), which now became a focal point for all aspects of parachuting. All matters relating to parachute operations, standardization, and training now originated from the CPC, whose great importance lies in its ability to perpetuate the skill and central doctrine of the airborne art and science.

Nonetheless, the three regimental parachute companies still represent the apex of light infantry soldiering. They are a beacon to the young, aggressive, motivated soldiers who seek challenges and a degree of hardship and experience not available in the mechanized infantry battalions. In recognition of this, and in testimony to their

Afghanistan, June 2002: a light machine gun team from A Coy (Para), 3 PPCLI Battle Group, lays down covering fire during a training exercise at Tarnac Farms near Kandahar. (Courtesy of photographer Capt J.Jasper)

quality, the parachute companies have consistently been relied on as the vanguard of their battalions, and of the Army when assigned the rapid reaction role. They have also been assigned the leading role in operations in complex terrain such as urban areas, deserts, jungles and mountains, as well as in Non-Combatant Evacuation Operations. Since 1995 the parachute companies have collectively established an enviable record of excellence, on domestic operations as well as overseas in such theatres as East Timor, Bosnia-Herzegovina and Afghanistan. They have consistently been tasked with difficult cordon and search operations, raids and patrolling in hostile areas or during complex coalition operations.

The PPCLI Para Coy participated with US forces on combat operations in Afghanistan in spring 2001 as part of Operation 'Harpoon' – an air assault into the 8,500-foot Terghul Gar mountains to

Zabol Province, Afghanistan, July 2002: signallers of A Coy (Para), 3 PPCLI BG man the Company Tactical Command Post during Operation 'Cherokee Sky' south of the Skinkay Valley. Note the new pixel-format CADPAT (TW) summer camouflage uniform. (Courtesy of Maj S.Hackett)

destroy any remaining Al Queda and Taliban resistance. Their combat loads, not including personal equipment, topped 120 pounds. They also deployed to the Tora Bora region as part of Operation 'Tor II' to deny the reoccupation of that vital ground to the enemy. Finally, they conducted combat operations in the Zabol region as part of Operation 'Cherokee Sky'.

* * *

In the end, Canada's airborne capability has evolved in step with the nation's political and

military circumstances and the international security environment. Although the various organizations have changed over the years, one factor has always remained constant – Canada's paratroopers have invariably represented the best of the country's combat soldiers, reflecting the values and qualities of a distinct warrior caste. Consistently, they have been recognized as the more adventurous, aggressive, motivated, and physically fit soldiers in the Army, and the 'can-do' attitude of paratroopers everywhere is a central tenet of their human and military character.

Kabul, Afghanistan, September 2003: paratroopers of Para Coy, 3 RCR, on foot patrol with a local counterpart. They wear CADPAT (TW) uniforms, wide brimmed combat hats and Canadian fragmentation protection vests. Due to the intense heat the paratroopers were issued with commercial 'Camelback' hydration daypacks. The man at front left has white plastic snap-ties for securing prisoners hanging from his equipment. (Courtesy 3 RCR Para Coy)

Kabul, Afghanistan, 2004: paratroopers of 3 R22eR Battalion Group patrol near the ruins of the King's Palace during Operation 'Athena'. The soldier in the foreground wears the tactical vest which replaces the 1982-pattern web equipment. He carries a TCCCS radio and a Global Positioning System, and slung from his shoulder is a 5.56mm C8 carbine with collapsible stock. (Photographer Frank Hudec, DND, CJIL, NEG# 2004-2050A)

55

Hurry up and wait...
(Courtesy CAFM)

THE PLATES

A: 1st CANADIAN PARACHUTE BATTALION

A1: Captain, service dress; Canada, 1942–45

While in Canada, officers wore the service dress jacket and plain trousers for ceremonial and social occasions, with brown leather shoes and the Sam Browne belt. Affixed to the maroon beret matching that of British Airborne Forces is the officers' bright brass version of the battalion's cap badge. Bronze metal rank 'pips' were worn on the shoulder straps of the jacket. Officers' collar badges were made of sterling silver. Officers were authorized to wear either the regular bright brass buttons or new Canadian Parachute Corps buttons. All battalion personnel wore the standard Canadian Parachute Qualification Badge – 'wings' – on the left breast. (For enlarged details of insignia featured on these plates, see Plate H.)

A2: Parachute candidate, Parachute School, Fort Benning, Georgia, USA, 1942–43

Canadian candidates were issued the school's standard olive drab 'satin' balloon cloth coveralls, Corcoran jump boots and, during the qualification jump stage, a clear plastic Riddell football helmet. The parachute system is the standard US T-5 backpack with chest-mounted reserve pack.

A3: Private, Camp Shilo, Manitoba, 1943

Standard 'battledress, serge' was made in Canada to the British 1937 pattern but of a rather superior cloth, in a slightly greener shade of khaki; throughout the war it retained the original fly front and pleated pockets. Successful parachute school candidates were awarded their 'wings', identical for all ranks. Following their return to Canada, in April 1943, all personnel were issued the new maroon beret with a brown plastic version of the battalion cap badge; a rifle-green 'AIRBORNE/ CANADA' shoulder title was also issued, and later '1/ CANADIAN PARACHUTE/ BATTALION' (see Plate H). In Europe, 1944–45, a gold-yellow loop was worn round the base of the BD shoulder straps to distinguish the battalion within the British 3rd Parachute Brigade. This soldier retains the Corcoran jump boots issued at Fort Benning.

B: 1st CANADIAN PARACHUTE BATTALION

B1: Private; North-West Europe, 1944–45

This soldier wears combat uniform and equipment, still with Corcoran jump boots. Battledress now included the special airborne troops' trousers with extra-large three-snap expanding pocket on the left thigh and two rear hip pockets. The third-type British airborne steel helmet has a plain turned rim, first-type black leather chin strapping and cup, and a camouflage net. The camouflage-printed British Denison smock displays the Canadian 'wings' on the breast. The British 37-pattern webbing equipment has green paint applied to give a textured camouflage pattern. The camouflage-printed mesh face veil was used in a variety of ways. The weapon is the .303in Lee-Enfield No.4 Mk I rifle.

B2: Private, Operation 'Varsity'; Germany, 1945
Guarding an Airspeed Horsa troop glider, this paratrooper wears essentially the same uniform and equipment. His helmet has the second-type chin strapping in khaki webbing. For extra warmth paratroopers were issued the standard sleeveless brown leather jerkin, worn over the Denison smock. He now wears standard issue black 'ammunition boots' with web anklets. The weapon is the 9mm Mk V (Airborne) Sten gun with wooden stock and forward pistol grip.

B3: Company Quartermaster Sergeant-Major, Germany, 1945
A new brass Other Ranks' version of the battalion cap badge was issued in late 1944–early 1945; apart from the material it was identical to the plastic type. This CQSM, riding a British lightweight Royal Enfield WD RE motorcycle, has also acquired brown leather despatch rider's gauntlets, a German rabbit-fur jacket, and a late model American .30cal M1A1 carbine with folding stock.

A PIAT anti-tank team at Lembeck, Germany, 29 March 1945. On the sergeant's battledress can be seen the battalion's distinctive gold-yellow shoulder strap loop, above the title '1/ CANADIAN PARACHUTE/ BATTALION', above the British Airborne Forces 'Pegasus' sleeve patch in pale blue on maroon. (Photographer Charlie H.Richer, LAC, PA-137325)

C: CANADIAN SPECIAL AIR SERVICE COMPANY & MOBILE STRIKING FORCE

C1: Private, Princess Patricia's Canadian Light Infantry Platoon, Canadian Special Air Service Company; Rivers, Manitoba, 1948
Post-war Canadian paratroopers still wore the British Denison smock with their World War II or post-war 'wings' on the left breast. The light khaki trousers are part of the Canadian Army's World War II Khaki Drill (Bush) uniform. The Cdn SAS Coy opted to use the American M-1C airborne troops' helmet rather than the British model, and Corcoran jump boots.

C2: Sergeant, Royal 22e Regiment, Mobile Striking Force; Rivers, Manitoba, 1950s
Due to the emphasis on the ostensible role of the MSF in defending the far North, paratroopers were issued with Canadian Army and RCAF winter uniforms and equipment. This R22eR sergeant wears the regular Army khaki drab service dress cap, an RCAF khaki drill flight overall with dark brown false fur collar, dark blue flying gloves, and standard Army black ankle boots.

C3: Private, Princess Patricia's Canadian Light Infantry, Mobile Striking Force; Rivers, Manitoba, 1950s
MSF paratroopers reverted to the World War II British Mk II (third-type) airborne helmet. The new olive-green drab (OG No.7) insulated nylon winter parka has an oversized fur-lined hood. The matching insulated trousers are worn over the uniform trousers for extra warmth. The mukluks – traditional-style winter boots – were made with a water-resistant white cotton material. This paratrooper wears the standard American T-10 main parachute and reserve. Operational doctrine dictated that they jump with their personal weapons, ammunition and rucksacks. The rifle valise rigged to the soldier's left leg protected the weapon during the jump and landing.

D: MOBILE STRIKING FORCE & DEFENCE OF CANADA FORCE

D1: Private, Royal Canadian Regiment, Mobile Striking Force; Camp Petawawa, Ontario, 1950s

The maroon beret dislays a metal RCR cap badge. The jacket and trousers are the post-World War II-pattern Khaki Drill (Bush) uniform, with the trouser cuffs secured over the black ankle boots by short khaki drab wool puttees. The paratrooper still wears 37-pattern webbing, and carries a Sten gun.

D2: Private, Royal Canadian Regiment, Mobile Striking Force; Toronto, Ontario, 1951

This paratrooper on the DZ removes his Sten from the 08/37-pattern large pack in which it was stowed during the jump. He wears the British World War II airborne troops' helmet with 1949-pattern OG No.7 Summer Field (Bush) Dress. The Canadian 37-pattern web equipment includes basic pouches, belt, braces, messtin stowed in a waterbottle carrier, and camouflage oilskin gas cape.

D3: Sergeant Jump Master, Canadian Joint Air Training Centre; Rivers, Manitoba, 1956

The British airborne helmet is painted maroon to differentiate CJATC staff from candidates. The new nylon parachutist's jump smock in OG No.7 has a full-length front zip fastener and black lift-a-dot snaps. He wears the olive-green trousers of the standard 1949-pattern Summer Field (Bush) Dress; the parachute is the American T.10 with back and reserve packs.

E: CANADIAN AIRBORNE REGIMENT

E1: Warrant Officer, UNFICYP; Cyprus, 1974

While serving on United Nations missions, Cdn AB Regt personnel wore the blue beret and UN badge. This shirtless warrant officer wears an American M-69 body armour 'flak vest', and the trousers of the olive-green Canadian combat uniform of nylon/cotton twist fabric, issued to the Army in 1963–64. His footwear is standard issue Mk II black leather laced high combat boots.

E2: Corporal; CFB Petawawa, Ontario, late 1970s

The maroon beret bears the Cdn AB Regt's bi-metal badge; the unit's unique bilingual composition was indicated by the scroll 'AIRBORNE/CANADA/AEROPORTÉ'. The first examples of this camouflaged jump smock resembling British DPM pattern were issued in 1975, and they were worn until the regiment's disbandment twenty years later; the colours are khaki tan, black, drab olive-green and dark brown. Again, the smock has a full-length front zipper and lift-a-dot snaps. Rank is displayed on shoulder strap slides, above a subdued title; subdued jump wings are worn on the chest, and the Special Service Force winged sword patch on both upper sleeves. This paratrooper wears the CT-1 main parachute and RS-1 reserve.

E3: Sergeant, service dress, 1968–86

Following the unpopular 1967 Canadian Forces Unification Act, all three services were issued the new CF Service Dress, Rifle Green; this was the uniform that was worn for ceremonial by the Cdn AB Regt at CFB Edmonton, Alberta – with the addition from 1976 of this Special Service Force sleeve patch

Mobile Striking Force officers of the Royal 22e Regiment wearing Summer Field (Bush) Dress during the 1950s. Dress regulations stipulated that the Canadian Parachute Qualification Badge and medalribbons be sewn on to a piece of Bush uniform material, fixed to the jacket with snaps. Unit shoulder titles also had to be temporarily fixed; here the blue/yellow/red arc of the 'Vingt-Deux', with white and black lettering, is sewn to armlets attached to the jacket or shirt shoulder straps and worn on both sleeves. The officers are wearing 1937-pattern web waist belts modified with regimental buckles. (Courtesy CAFM)

During the 1970s and 1980s very few modifications were made to the Canadian combat uniform. This sergeant – note subdued rank badges on both sleeves – carries a C-77 radio set over his 1964-pattern webbing Fighting Order, and is armed with the 7.62mm FNC1A1 self-loading rifle. (Courtesy CAFM)

– and in the 1980s at CFB Petawawa, Ontario. It is worn here with bright buttons bearing the regimental insignia; all-ranks' collar badges based on the design worn by officers in World War II; and maroon-and-gold shoulder titles. The white maple leaf on the Canadian Parachute Qualification Badge denoted service with an operational airborne unit. The uniform is set off by the infantry senior NCO's traditional scarlet shoulder sash; a white plastic ceremonial belt with a gold-coloured buckle plate to which a regimental cap badge is soldered; and black SSF parade boots. The weapon is the 7.62mm FN C1A1 self-loading (semi-automatic) rifle.

F: CANADIAN AIRBORNE REGIMENT
F1: Master/Corporal Pathfinder; CFB Petawawa, Ontario, 1980s
The regiment's pathfinders were qualified for high altitude/low opening (HALO) operational insertions. This

paratrooper is prepared for such a jump with a black plastic helmet, goggles, and a wool face mask for protection and warmth during the free fall from high altitude. He wears an OG No.7 fleece turtleneck sweater under a combat dress shirt, jacket and trousers, a pair of mukluks, and regular black leather combat gloves. He is equipped with the 7-TU Freefall parachute system, and a wrist altimeter.

F2: LMG gunner, UNITAF; Somalia, 1993
During their deployment to the Horn of Africa the Cdn AB Regt wore their green combat uniforms with a red-and-white national shoulder flash. New items such as the wide-brim 'Tilley' hat and American tan desert boots were issued in-theatre. This paratrooper has the 1982-pattern OG No.7 web equipment Fighting Order, and carries a 5.56mm C9A1 light machine gun with optical sight.

1985: Front and rear views of the CT-1 main and RS-1 reserve parachutes – see Plate E2; the static line is bright yellow. Rigged below the reserve pack is the paratrooper's C-2 Universal Rucksack. (Courtesy CAFM)

OPPOSITE **Men of 3 RCR's Parachute Company, c.2003. In the foreground, note the new Canadian Army Disruptive Pattern (CADPAT) Temperate Woodland (TW) uniform in pixel pattern – see Plate G3; the new CG 634 helmet, 1982-pattern webbing in Battle Order, and a Model 870P Remington 12-gauge pump shotgun. The paratrooper in the background wears the new model Coat, Combat, Improved Environmental Clothing System (IECS), and carries a 5.56mm C7A1 rifle equipped with a 40mm M-203A1 grenade launcher. (Courtesy CAFM)**

F3: Major, summer service dress; CFB Petawawa, Ontario, 1994

In 1985 the CF reverted to distinctive uniforms for the Army, Navy and Air Force. The Army used the new pattern of Service Dress, Rifle Green, Land as its winter uniform, and introduced this Service Dress, Tan, DEU for summer. The material was of a heavier weave and the jacket featured shoulder straps. On the maroon beret this major wears an officers' embroidered wire regimental cap badge. The jacket has bright brass-coloured regimental buttons, and a new gold-coloured metal regimental shoulder strap title, above a woven 'CANADA' shoulder title in gold-yellow on green. Note the gold-and-dark green rank rings around the cuffs. For ceremonial dress the officer wears a white sword belt, white gloves, and his full decorations.

G: PARACHUTE COMPANIES

G1: Corporal, Parachute Company, 3rd Battalion Royal Canadian Regiment – Light Infantry; CFB Petawawa, Ontario, 1996

For winter operations this soldier wears a white wool toque, and the X53 white nylon camouflage coat and trousers over his CADPAT (TW) winter combat dress. The insulated winter mitts are made from pliable leather and nylon. The footwear is a pair of waterproofed, insulated nylon mukluks. The weapon is the 7.62mm C6 General Purpose Machine Gun.

G2: Sergeant, Parachute Company, 3rd Battalion Royal 22e Regiment – Light Infantry; East Timor, 1999

This was the last operational deployment in which paratroopers used the olive-green combat shirt and trousers. This NCO wears 1982-pattern web equipment Fighting Order, with a privately purchased chest magazine carrier – note the sergeant's rank tab – and an issued commercial 'Camelback' hydration daypack. He carries the 5.56mm C7A1 rifle with optical sight.

G3: Corporal, Parachute Company, 3rd Battalion Royal Canadian Regiment – Light Infantry; Afghanistan, 2003

The paratrooper wears a CADPAT (TW) summer hat, jacket and trousers; this latest combat uniform was issued to Canadian Forces personnel in 2001. The predominant colour is olive-green with a pixel-format camouflage pattern of dark green, black and brown. On his left arm brassard are sewn a Canadian flag flash, above the insignia of the International Security Assistance Force (ISAF) and Kabul Multinational Brigade (KMNB). He also wears body armour; the new CF Tactical Vest (TV) which replaced the traditional webbing equipment; and a pair of Goretex Wet Weather Boots (WWB). His radio is the Tactical Command, Control and Communication System (TCCCS), and he is armed with a 5.56mm C7A1 rifle.

H: CANADIAN AIRBORNE INSIGNIA, 1942–95

H1: 1st Cdn Para Bn Other Ranks' cap badge, brown plastic
H2: World War II embroidered Canadian Parachute Qualification Badge
H3: 1 Cdn Para Bn printed shoulder title
H4: 1 Cdn Para Bn embroidered shoulder title
H5: 1 Cdn Para Bn officers' collar badge; the Latin motto stamped on the cloud is 'EX COELIS' – 'Out of the Clouds'

H6: Cdn AB Regt bi-metal cap badge

H7: Cdn AB Regt bullion Canadian Parachute Qualification Badge with metal maple leaf

H8: Cdn AB Regt 'Swiss' embroidered shoulder title, worn with Service Dress, Rifle Green, Canadian Forces, 1969–87

H9: Cdn AB Regt 'Swiss' embroidered shoulder title, worn on shoulder strap slides of Combat Dress

H10: 1 Cdn Para Bn service dress button, large

H11: Cdn AB Regt officers's wire-embroidered beret badge

H12: Cdn AB Regt all ranks' 'Swiss' embroidered badge for Combat Field Cap

H13: 'Swiss' embroidered Special Service Force sleeve patch, worn on jump smock; the motto is 'OSONS' – ' We Dare'

H14: Cdn AB Regt 'Swiss' embroidered Canadian Parachute Qualification Badge with white maple leaf, worn on jump smock

H15: Cdn AB Regt metal shoulder title worn on the Service Dress, Land, and the Service Dress, Distinctive Environmental Uniform (DEU), Tan, 1987–95

H16: Cdn AB Regt tunic button, small, worn on Service Dress, Land, and Service Dress, DEU, Tan

H17: Cdn AB Regt all ranks' collar badge, worn on Service Dress

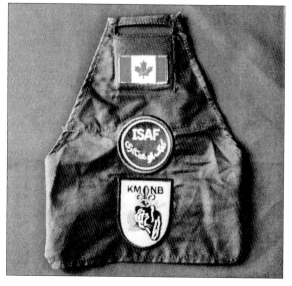

Detail of Plate G3. Below the red-and-white national flash are the insignia of the International Security Assistance Force (ISAF), in white on emerald green; and the Kabul Multinational Brigade – black and white tiger head and fleur-de-lys, black 'KM NB', on a pale tan 'map', all on off-white shield, edged black. (Courtesy Daniel Côté)

INDEX